FRAME OF MIND

THE AUTOBIOGRAPHY OF THE WORLD SNOOKER CHAMPION

FRAME OF MIND

THE AUTOBIOGRAPHY OF THE WORLD SNOOKER CHAMPION

GRAEME DOTT

with Derek Clements

JOHN BLAKE

Published by John Blake Publishing Ltd,
3 Bramber Court, 2 Bramber Road,
London W14 9PB, England

www.johnblakepublishing.co.uk

First published in hardback in 2011

ISBN: 9781843583462

British Library Cataloguing-in-Publication Data:

A catalogue record for this book is available from the British Library.

Design by www.envydesign.co.uk

Printed in Great Britain by CPI Mackays, Chatham ME5 8TD

1 3 5 7 9 10 8 6 4 2

Papers used by John Blake Publishing are natural, recyclable products made from wood grown in sustainable forests. The manufacturing processes conform to the environmental regulations of the country of origin.

All images from the author's collection except where indicated

I dedicate this book to Alex Lambie. Without him I would never have achieved a fraction of what I have managed to do. He backed me, he supported me and he gave me the confidence and self-belief to play snooker at the highest level. He was one of the kindest men I ever had the privilege of meeting and he died far, far too young.

And without Alex in my life, there would have been no Elaine. I owe her a special thank you for being such a wonderful wife and fantastic mother. She was my rock when I was at my lowest and my best friend through all the highs and lows. I know that it could not have been easy for her when my depression was at its worst but through it all she offered nothing but support and love. She stood by me and we came through it. Now our family is complete with our children, Lewis and Lucy and we could not be happier.

I also want to say thank to Mum, Dad, Uncle George, my brothers John and Billy, my friends Jim and Alexander and to everybody else who has helped me throughout my life, on and off the snooker table.

CONTENTS

FOREWORD

Graeme Dott is one of the most delightful people I have ever had the pleasure of meeting. He is a credit to himself, to his family and to the game of snooker.

I first came across him many years ago when he was struggling with his game and came down to Wales to see me. We sat down and spoke for hours. It was obvious to me that there wasn't much wrong with Graeme's game but, like many players before and since, he had reached the point where he had almost lost the will to play the game because he wasn't producing the results he knew he was capable of.

Sport is like that. When you are at the top of your game, you can't wait to get out there and do your thing, whether it be football, tennis, golf, snooker or whatever. But when your confidence takes a knock, it can start to affect all sorts of things.

One of the key things that Graeme and I worked on was motivation. I realised that he was a very competitive individual and that, if he could get his preparation and his motivation sorted out, he would soon start winning matches again and, when he did that, so his confidence would return.

Graeme may say that I unlocked something in him and the results were pretty immediate because within a matter of weeks he had reached his first final and made a maximum break, winning himself a car in the process. The truth is that Graeme did it all himself.

And he also did it all himself when he went on to win the World Championship. I listen to people talking about talented and gifted snooker players – it was said for years that Jimmy White was the most talented player ever to pick up a snooker cue but, in my mind, talent is all about winning. Graeme Dott is a winner, and I can't tell you how delighted I was when he won the World Championship.

He went through some very dark days and difficult times when his father-in-law died, and it is to his eternal credit that he has come out the other side. It cannot have been easy for him.

To be honest, I thought that his form, when he lost in the final of the 2010 World Championship, was better than when he won it. Many so-called gifted players have never been world champion – it takes special qualities to reach that status; qualities that Graeme possesses in spades.

Some pundits suggest that he is not the most fluent of players, but he is certainly one of the most determined. He looks as if he is trying his heart out on every shot that he plays and I have always believed that, if you say that about yourself, you can go home and sleep easy at night.

X

I love watching Graeme play. It is great to see him back among the game's elite and it looks to me that he is ready to start winning again. His story is an inspirational one and I can't wait to read it.

Terry Griffiths

PROLOGUE

OPENING BREAK

I was sitting in class one day and Mrs McDonald, a teacher I didn't get on with, was talking about forthcoming exams. She was really winding me up, and eventually I said, 'Listen, I don't care about the exams.'

'Don't be silly,' she said. 'Why don't you care about them, Graeme?'

'Because I am not going to be sitting them. I am going to be leaving school.'

'And what are you planning to do with the rest of your life?'

'I am going to become a professional snooker player.'

'Graeme, you will never make a living as a snooker player.'

I remember her words very clearly. She had obviously never heard of Stephen Hendry and was oblivious to the explosion of interest in snooker that he had generated. Alan McManus, John Higgins, Drew Henry... There was a production line churning out top players. Finally, it seemed, Scotland had found a sport that it could dominate.

And I wanted to be part of that production line. Stephen was setting new standards, breaking records all over the place and earning lots of money. He was an exciting player. It seemed that every time he got in among the balls he would score a century.

Despite Mrs McDonald's words, I knew that I could play a bit. I was winning junior and amateur tournaments all over the country, and receiving positive publicity, which delighted the likes of the headmaster at Lochend, my secondary school. It was just a shame that Mrs McDonald did not agree with my chosen career path, whereas some teachers'
encouragement can stay with you for your whole life.

I remember having to pick a subject in third year to make up the numbers for my GCSEs and I opted for photography. To be honest, I thought it would be a good opportunity to have a bit of a laugh, and I was really looking forward to it until I walked into my first lesson and there was Mrs McDonald. How did that happen?

Don't get me wrong. She wasn't a bad teacher, she didn't mistreat me and I didn't hate her, but I just couldn't relate to her. And what right did she have to tell me that I wouldn't make it as a snooker player anyway?

At least my parents, my brothers and my uncle George all seemed to believe that I could make a decent living from the game. Later, the support of Alex Lambie (my manager) and his daughter Elaine would also be invaluable.

Yet, in their own way, Mrs McDonald's words had encouraged me in an unexpected way. She had made me absolutely determined to prove her wrong.

CHAPTER ONE

ROUGH WITH THE SMOOTH

I was born in Easterhouse on 12 May 1977 into a traditional working-class Glasgow family: my father John, my mother Susan and three older brothers, John, Robert and Billy. I was the baby of the family, the last chance for a girl, but it didn't happen.

As you will discover, I grew up in a pretty tough area and knowing that I could call on my brothers if I needed to was extremely useful. It meant that I didn't get into much trouble.

My grandfather, my dad and my uncle have all, at some time, worked for Yarrows, the shipbuilders on the River Clyde. For much of the 20th century there was a huge workforce employed on the Clyde and the yards built some of the world's most famous liners, including the QE2.

Most of the men who worked there had what were regarded as jobs for life and their sons would follow them into the shipyards. For years it provided a working wage for thousands of Glaswegian men. The work was demanding but the guys also had plenty of fun. Billy Connolly, the Big Yin, worked in the shipyards on the Clyde and it was there he met many of the characters who formed the basis for much of his early comedy work.

When Dad left Yarrows, it was to work in a giant refrigeration unit. It would be fair to say that the majority of the men knew how to look after themselves – in order to survive in that environment, you had to. They would receive their weekly pay packet and then head off to the pub for a few drinks on a Friday night and, hopefully, when they got home there would still be some money to give to their wives. These men worked hard all week but they played hard too, my dad among them.

It is important that you understand what Easterhouse was like – and still is to a large extent. I suppose that it would be classed as a housing estate but that doesn't begin to do it justice. In Scotland we call them housing 'schemes', and I guess that the majority of the people who lived there would believe that the Corporation of Glasgow had a 'scheme' to create just about the worst possible living conditions you could imagine.

Nowadays, Easterhouse has a population of nearly 30,000 (in the early 1960s it had been almost double that figure) and, in anybody's book, that is a big housing estate. It would have been fine if the housing stock was up to standard and the amenities were adequate enough to cope with the size of the place but both fell way short of the mark. Unemployment was rampant and there were also lots of health issues; I guess that so many people were unhealthy because they ate rubbish and that included lots of fried food, floating in grease. Glasgow was known as the heart-attack capital of Europe and Easterhouse led the way, for all the wrong reasons.

The area was littered with tenement buildings, with communal entrances, many of which always seemed to smell of urine. Our house had three bedrooms, so there was never a lot of space. We had no garden but that was OK – if you live in a multi-storey tenement, you don't expect to have a garden, and at least there was no shortage of grassy areas where we could kick a football.

But almost no one had a car – it would have lasted about five minutes before somebody would have stolen or vandalised it. Even today, one of the most striking features about walking through Easterhouse is how few people seem to own cars.

There were hardly any shops either and the ones that did serve Easterhouse were stuck on the outskirts of the estate, which meant that families often had to walk miles for their shopping. If we had to make a journey, it was either by bus or on foot. There were all sorts of problems with having to trek to the shops, one of which was when you would arrive home to discover that you had forgotten to buy some milk or butter. And so somebody would have to walk all the way back.

To give you an idea of how rough the area was, when we went out with Mum she always made a point, after a hundred yards or so, of looking back towards our house and waving. I would say, 'Mum, there's nobody in.'

'I know that Graeme, but you see all those boys over there? If they see me waving they will think there's still somebody at home and they won't break in.'

It really was as bad as that.

It didn't register with me at the time but there wasn't a library either. Not that I would have used it because the only thing that interested me as a child was playing football and supporting Rangers.

You need to know something about being a football supporter in Glasgow. There is a religious divide in the city and it shows no sign of disappearing. If you are born as a Protestant, you support Rangers. If you are a Roman Catholic, you support Celtic. Period. There is no middle ground. Go to an Old Firm match between the two rival sides and, despite the best efforts of both clubs to change things, you will hear sectarian songs, with Rangers fans making reference to William of Orange and screaming, 'Fuck the Pope.' As a lifelong Rangers supporter, what any of this has to do with football I have absolutely no idea.

All the same, these attitudes are entrenched. My dad is a fanatical Rangers fan but, when Graeme Souness was manager of the club and signed Mo Johnston in 1989, he went ballistic, threw his season ticket away and vowed never again to set foot in Ibrox, home to the club's ground. 'That is a disgrace,' he said. Johnston, you see, was not only a Catholic but had played for the dreaded Celtic. It was headline news in Scotland for days – as a 12-year-old, I remember watching a news broadcast showing a supporter walking up to the ground and handing his season ticket back in disgust. I cannot begin to imagine the inner turmoil Johnston must have gone through. Of course, it is true that he was being paid a great deal of money, but he could have had his pick of clubs and I choose to believe that what he did took some courage and some balls.

I was just delighted that Rangers had signed a great striker who would score lots of goals – and so he did. There were a couple of games against Celtic in which Johnston, who must have felt under incredible pressure, missed chances that he would normally have tucked away. 'There you go, what did I tell you? He's missing those deliberately,' said Dad.

Dad did eventually swallow his pride and returned to Ibrox to support the club but many others in those dark ages did not. I continue to believe that Souness is to be commended for his actions. A player's religion should not matter, just as the colour of his skin should not be a consideration. It is a subject that I will return to later because it very nearly cost me my life.

The religious split also extends to the schools. My primary school was called Commonhead and to get to it I had to walk past a Roman Catholic school called St Collette's. I would regularly have stones thrown at me when I got anywhere near the place. Of course, this wasn't pleasant but I didn't know any better. It was just the way it was.

A golden opportunity arose for religious barriers to be broken down while I was still a pupil at Commonhead Primary. When St Colette's school was damaged in a fire – which I remain convinced was started deliberately – hundreds of its pupils had no school to attend. A meeting was arranged at Commonhead but it was hijacked by a leading Catholic activist, who demanded that all us Protestant children be removed and sent elsewhere so that the St Colette's kids could take over our school.

Needless to say, that did not go down too well with our parents, the majority of whom were prepared to extend the hand of friendship and compromise. Why couldn't the children all mix and attend the school together? Well, that was never going to happen. In the end, the Catholic children did come to our school for a few months but they had their own assembly in the morning and their own lessons. And we didn't mix with them at break time either. It was an opportunity wasted.

One of my greatest moments as a schoolboy came when I played football for Commonhead against St Colette's. Apart from myself and one other boy, we had an absolutely useless team. Every week we would play against other schools and every week we would get a right good hiding. It was embarrassing. With no tactics or skill, every match that we played usually seemed to involve all 20 outfield players chasing the ball all over the pitch.

Luckily, St Colette's team was even worse than ours. So on this glorious, never-to-be-forgotten occasion, we beat our deadly local rivals 3-2, and I managed to score a hat-trick. What made it better still was the fact that there were a lot of parents on the touchline. I don't think we ever managed to win another game though.

You may find the following story hard to believe but I swear it is true. My secondary school was called Lochend and it was only a matter of yards away from the Catholic school, St Leonard's. In an effort to keep the kids away from each other, one school would open 15 minutes before the other and would close 15 minutes earlier. It didn't work, of course, and it was bonkers to think that it would. The kids just used to hang around and wait for the other school to get out and fights would then begin.

I look back now and find it incredible that the powers-that-be felt it was necessary to have these staggered finishing times.

Why couldn't we all just get along with each other? The reality was that they wanted to beat our brains in and we wanted to do the same to them but, if you had sat those kids down and asked them why they detested each other, I guarantee that they would not have been able to provide a sensible answer, only a shrug of, 'Just because...'

There were lots of no-go areas in Easterhouse; streets you would avoid by taking huge detours because they were the personal and private property of the gangs who lived there. You would never want to find out what might happen to you if you strayed into one of these areas.

Lots of people have tried to solve the problems in Easterhouse. Singer Frankie Vaughan famously tried to act as a mediator in the late 1960s, when the rivalry between the gangs flared out of control. Violence was commonplace and the weapon of choice was the knife. Vaughan launched the Easterhouse Project in 1968, a scheme that was still flourishing when he died in 1999. He managed to persuade a number of gangs to hand their weapons over to the police. Positive noises were made and gang members even took to the streets to start clearing graffiti from the walls, but the peace did not last long.

Drummy, Toi, Den Toi, Bal Toi, Aggro, Skinheads, Bar-L, Pak, Rebels – they were just some of the gangs that struck fear and terror into the estate. I often wonder, even now, what went through the minds of my mother and the parents of the other children I was friendly with whenever we were late home. Mum hated living in Easterhouse with a passion. She hated the house we lived in and she hated everything about the area.

Iain Duncan Smith, the former leader of the Conservative Party, was appalled by what he found when he first visited Easterhouse, and pledged to do something to try to put things right, but I wonder if anybody can ever really solve the problems. There is high unemployment, drug and alcohol abuse, teenage pregnancy, and the kids underachieve at school, so what chance do they have?

Many of the houses have now been demolished, including my old home. Others lie derelict and boarded up. And on a recent trip back there I was broken-hearted to see football pitches left untended, with the grass overgrown and the goal posts rusting away. I was lucky: while we used to come home from school and then go out and kick a ball about, it seems that today's Easterhouse kids either sit at home playing computer games or hang around on street corners. It is fair to say that some facilities have improved – now there are sports centres and suchlike – but I wonder if the local kids use them.

My school days, though, were not especially happy. I wasn't bullied or anything like that – I just hated school, especially Lochend. I was not great at lessons and I knew from an early age that I was going to make my living by playing snooker. I was much better at PE, especially football and basketball. Lochend's football team was even worse than Commonhead's, but we were one of the best teams in Scotland, never mind Glasgow. I know it seems odd because, when you think of Scottish sport, basketball is not something that readily springs to mind, but we were the business.

Throughout my time at Lochend, I always had a good relationship with my PE teachers. Whenever we tried a new sport, I would always be the boy who was singled out to demonstrate to the others how it should be done. It helped that I enjoyed it but I guess that I was a natural at most sports. Best of all, the teachers also showed a genuine interest in what I was doing on the snooker table.

Lochend was rough nonetheless; the sort of place where even the bullies were bullied. And the actual buildings were incredibly depressing, with damp in the classrooms, paint peeling off window ledges and windows being broken on a fairly regular basis. Eventually the school buildings were demolished and rebuilt about 300 yards away. Vastly improved, it now boasts a state-of-the-art building with the most modernised facilities.

I was pretty streetwise from a very early age and I guess that I just worked out a way to keep my head down, play my cards close to my chest and keep out of trouble. When I walked home from school I would take a different route home most days. It sounds bizarre now but I didn't give it a second thought. This area was controlled by this gang, another area was controlled by that gang and, if you were caught 'trespassing' on uncharted territory, you would have to run for your life. I dread to think what might have happened to me if I had ever taken a wrong turning and strayed into uncharted territory. You just didn't do it. If I had wanted to take a short cut, I would have had to accept that it came with a good kicking.

The problem with Lochend in those days, and maybe even now, is that members of all the gangs I mentioned earlier attended the school, which meant the rivalry was constant. Fights would kick off all the time for no discernible reason. In many ways, it was like being in prison. You had to avoid certain people and you had to be careful about who you were seen talking to – if you were seen having a laugh with the 'wrong' people, Heaven help you. It all sounds very primitive and it was, but my friends and I thought nothing of it because it was part and parcel of growing up in Easterhouse. I witnessed some massive fights, all arms and legs, boys (and girls) screaming and swearing at each other, blood everywhere. You can forget about the Marquess of Queensberry Rules too – they had no second thoughts about kicking people in the head and, of course, there were the knives.

When I was 13 we moved to Dennistoun. Mum had been trying for years to persuade the council to move us, saying that she needed to be closer to her own mother, in order to look after her. Mum would have done just about anything to get out of Easterhouse and it was a day of celebration when the council informed her that there was a place for us at Dennistoun, but it left me with some hard choices to make: Dennistoun is about ten miles from Easterhouse. It sounds daft looking back but I told Mum that I wanted to stay at Lochend, as my friends were at the school and I wanted to finish my studies, such as they were.

This presented me with a whole new challenge though. Walking home was out of the question – not only was it much too far but the journey would once again have taken me through some no-go areas. It meant that I always had to ensure I had my bus fare with me and that was a challenge in itself because there was always somebody who would be ready to try and snatch it from you.

Then there was the route itself. On one occasion I was half asleep at the back of the bus and minding my own business.

As the bus slowed down I was aware of somebody forcing open the emergency door from the outside, making a grab for me and trying to punch me – all because I was in a part of Easterhouse where I wasn't supposed to be. Can you imagine how frightening that sort of thing is? Fortunately, I managed to break free and the driver pulled away, but it was the last time I ever sat beside the emergency door and the last time I even considered a nap on my homeward journey.

Even the act of catching the bus was an art in itself. There was a stop right outside the school but getting on with other pupils was a risk, as I could have been thrown off the bus if misbehaviour broke out. It would have been no problem for the others because they lived nearby but I'd have faced a long walk home because I never had any spare money. So every day, when the school bell rang, I would walk with one of my friends back to the area where I used to live in Easterhouse. It took about 15 minutes and by that time everybody else had caught their buses and gone home or been thrown off so, effectively, the coast was clear for me.

When I was about 16, by which time we had been in Dennistoun for about 3 years, my parents split up. Their relationship had deteriorated into constant arguments so it was decided it would be best if they went their separate ways. Dad ended up moving into his own council property but he remained in Dennistoun, not far from where Mum and I lived.

CHAPTER TWO

THE POCKET ROCKET

When I was about eight years old I got a half-size snooker table for Christmas. This was a huge deal for me because my family never had a great deal of money, and this table quickly became my pride and joy.

My uncle, George Cartledge, is my mother's younger brother and he became a central figure in my life at a very early age. George used to play snooker every Saturday with my late grandfather, Robert, at a club called Snooker Scene and I would constantly pester them to take me with them. Robert had bad legs. He would walk to the snooker club but would have to stop regularly to ease the pain and to get his breath back. Eventually his legs got so bad that he could no longer make it to the club.

It has to be said that the snooker clubs in Glasgow in those days were not places you would want to take your children. I am not sure that a lot of them are very much better today.

They smell of sweat and stale beer, and some people would say that the threat of menace hangs in the air, but the key is to keep yourself to yourself. Yes, dodgy characters play snooker but you could say the same thing about any sport.

George loved his snooker and I was pretty close to both him and my grandfather. He lived in Parkhead, not far from where the dreaded Celtic played their football and sometimes, after school on Fridays, I would get on the bus and go to spend the weekend with George. Naturally, I would turn a blind eye to the nearby football stadium.

There were dozens of snooker tables at Snooker Scene and, originally, I was only allowed to watch and to place the balls on the table, but I revelled in the experience all the same. When my grandfather's playing days came to an end, I constantly pestered George to take me to the club so that I could play with him. 'Can I go with you, Uncle George? Please take me. Please take me. Go on...'

Eventually he gave in and now my Saturday routine involved playing with him. I never wanted those sessions to end and he had to drag me off the table and back home for lunch. If I had been left to my own devices, I probably would have stayed there until they threw me out. I loved potting balls, making breaks and trying to get better.

I don't remember this but, apparently, the first time I ever played on a full-size table, George moved some balls about and told me to see what I could do. If I am small now (about 5ft 6in), I was really diminutive back then and struggled to reach the table. But with George and my grandfather looking on, I made a 40 break. Of course, I didn't understand the significance of what I had done, which may explain why I don't remember, but they most certainly did. At that stage, I wouldn't have had the first idea how to apply side or how to screw the ball, so that break was just down to pure instinct. So Uncle George must have realised he might be watching a boy who possessed some genuine natural talent, and he has since told me of the growing shared sense of amazement they had as I moved around that table potting snooker balls.

I played on the small table at home as often as I could, beating my brothers as a matter of course. At first they may have let me win but it wasn't long before they were trying their hardest and discovering that it wasn't good enough.

During one spell of hot summer weather, when I was only nine or ten and we were still living in Easterhouse, somebody in our tenement building had taken a six-foot snooker table outside (as you do) and set it up on the pavement so that the local men could play one another. I looked out the window and saw them. As you can imagine, within a matter of minutes I had legged it downstairs and started nagging the men. 'Can I get a game, mister? Please, can I get a shot?' They ignored me and were not going to let me play until eventually somebody said, 'For fuck's sake, give the wee guy a game.'

Just as with Uncle George, I had finally ground them down but they quickly came to regret it. If you won a frame, you stayed on the table and, once I was on, they couldn't get me off. I won frame after frame, winning constantly. Eventually Mum called down, 'Graeme, you will need to come in now. Your dinner is ready.'

Everybody cheered her. 'Thank God for that. Maybe somebody else can get a game now!'

I must have had some sort of eye for the game but I didn't

know it then, only that it was fun to win against other people, especially those who were so much older than me. What sticks in my mind is the reaction I used to get from people. I would play a shot without thinking about it and they would praise me, or I would hear an opponent saying, 'This boy is really good at this game, you know.' When you are young it gives you a real boost to get plaudits from your elders and it did wonders for my confidence.

I used to play on my half-size table in my bedroom. I also had a small black and white television set and, when the snooker was on, I would prop it up on a pillow so that I could watch as I played. I vividly remember doing precisely that in 1986 when Joe Johnson caused a sensation by beating Steve Davis in the final of the World Championship at The Crucible in Sheffield. I was just trying to copy my heroes, imagining that I was playing them for the world title, in precisely the same way that kids who play golf stand over a putt and think, I've got this one to win The Open.

As I was growing up, Davis was the dominant player in the game. Some people might think that I took up snooker because of Davis, or that it was due to watching Stephen Hendry come along and win everything in sight. While it might be romantic to say that was the case, I started playing snooker simply because I liked it.

I believe that everybody has a gift and the secret is to discover what your gift or talent might be. I feel sorry that some people go through their whole lives without finding what they excel at. Snooker came easily to me right from the off, although I can put my hand on my heart and tell you that at no stage in those early years did I think I could become a champion. The other thing is that I had a seriously suspect cue action. Because I had to compensate for being so small, my hand position was all wrong and my elbow stuck out, but I could still pot balls. I was unaware then, of course, that I would have to change my cue action at some stage if I was to make serious progress in the sport.

My parents and Uncle George knew of my potential and I am certain they would have thought about getting some professional coaching for me when I stopped growing. In the meantime, though, they encouraged me to start entering some junior snooker tournaments.

I made my first century break when I was 13 years old during one of my Saturday morning sessions playing with George. It was a wonderful feeling but what stays with me to this day is his reaction: he was bursting with pride and wanted to tell everybody he met that his little nephew had just scored 138 on a full-size snooker table. Prior to that, I'd had many chances to reach a century break but kept stopping in the 90s just short of the target. On that particular day, though, the pockets seemed like buckets to me and I couldn't miss.

I made that break at Dee Bee's snooker club in Dennistoun. When we first moved to that area we were told that a club was about to open and I couldn't believe my luck when it finally did – it was so close to where we lived that I could see it from our window. I used to play there with a guy called Aldo Brown, who was a fabulous snooker player – one day he had four tons or centuries in a row against me and you don't do that unless you can play a bit. It may astonish you to learn that, despite such capabilities, Aldo never contemplated turning professional but he worried that he would struggle under pressure and, besides, he thought that drink and women were more attractive options. When Aldo and I started playing together he would give me a head start of 40 but, before long, we began each frame equal.

We saw a junior tournament advertised in the local paper and decided to have a go. It was held at Reardon's Snooker Centre in Stockwell Street, Glasgow, on a Sunday morning and, lo and behold, I won all four matches and picked up £6 (don't ask me why it was such a strange amount) and a trophy. It turned out that the club regularly staged competitions for juniors, and I played in them as often as I could and soon found that I was doing well and winning regularly. By now the local papers were showing an interest but the only thing that interested me then was potting balls.

After I had played in a few tournaments at Reardon's, George felt that I might be ready to step up a level so he entered me in a pro-am at the Masters Club in Dennistoun. The club was located at the top of a very steep hill. In those days, George would hail a taxi for the two of us. The driver would set off up the hill then blow his top when told by George that we only wanted to go to the snooker club.

The pro-am brought together professionals and amateur players, using a handicap system it shared with golf. So, for example, if I was given a handicap of 30 and I was playing the best professional, who might be -5, it meant that he would have to give me a start of 35 in each frame. As you start to win matches, your handicap is reduced. The great thing about this format was that it allowed a totally average club player to compete against a professional and, maybe, just maybe, walk off with the prize. Occasionally this happened but, for the most part, it was the top players who won such games.

As I progressed in these tournaments, reaching the last eight and the occasional semi-final, my handicap was cut. I would moan to George that my handicap had been reduced to 20 but he would point out that this was a sign that I was actually getting better and that I should just try harder.

There were all sorts of logistical problems involved. I was still living in Easterhouse at the time and I never had any money, so it was always a constant struggle, even just to find the bus fares and the entrance fees to get into these competitions. As a kid I didn't realise just how hard my family's financial situation was. When you are 10, 11, 12, you just want, want, want and it was only years later that I discovered that Mum and the rest of the family had all pitched in together to scrape the money together for me to enter these tournaments. There was no silver spoon in my mouth or, indeed, in the mouths of any members of my family. Everything we got we had to work for.

Mum, Dad, Uncle George, my grandfather, aunts and my brothers – I have to thank them all for the financial contributions they made, although I did not realise it at the time. Please don't think that I was a spoilt brat because I believe that really wasn't the case, but they encouraged me to play, so I would just hold out my hand and ask for whatever money I required and, usually, they would find a way to provide it.

When I think about it now, all the pieces fit into place. It was really hard for my parents but they believed in my talent and were curious as to where it could take me. Maybe they never thought about how much money I could make in the professional game. They were just happy to see me doing something I enjoyed, content in the knowledge that they knew where I was and that I wasn't getting into any trouble.

And the more I played, the better I became. Soon I knew that I couldn't go on playing in Reardon's Sunday tournaments for ever. The next step was to compete on the Scottish amateur and junior circuits, where I was pitted against some of the most outstanding amateur snooker players in the country, as well as a couple of ex-professional guys who had returned to the unpaid ranks.

One week I might have played in the Scottish Under-18s Championship, the next it might have been the Scottish Amateur Championship but, whatever the tournament, almost without exception, I was competing against people who were far older than me. These guys knew how to play proper match snooker and it was a tremendous learning experience.

I believe that you probably learn more from the matches you lose than you do from the ones you win and, as a professional sportsman, you need to find out how to cope with defeat because the nature of the beast is that you lose more often than you win. When Stephen Hendry first arrived on the scene he found himself being touted as a future world champion and players such as Willie Thorne and Steve Davis were generous in their praise of him after beating him. All the while, though, even in defeat, Hendry was taking it all in and learning from the experience. He realised that he hated losing, which simply made him more determined not to be beaten any more. Roger Federer, Rafa Nadal and Tiger Woods are all built the same way.

Stepping up to play with the big boys meant that I had to travel. Some of the tournaments were played in Glasgow but most were not. At about this time, Uncle George was made redundant but he received a decent pay-off and he spent a lot of it helping me to travel to events. He told me that playing in Scottish tournaments was one thing but that I should also test myself against the best British players, and so it was that we found ourselves in places such as the North Wales resort of Prestatyn, where they staged snooker festivals. I would be a regular visitor to the town, as were many of my fellow competitors.

For many years Prestatyn was the location for countless qualifying matches for the big professional events. Anybody who thinks that the life of a snooker player is glamorous should spend some time at the qualifiers. They bring together a combination of hungry young stars and a group of players who have climbed the heights but find their powers on the wane and continue to rage against the dying of the fire. Tony Knowles, Kirk Stevens, John Parrott, Jimmy White, Steve Davis and Tony Drago have all been there. When you have tasted glory and played any sport at the highest level it is only natural that you want more, that you want it back, but the qualifiers are a soul-destroying existence.

If you have to be there, it is either because you are trying to progress from the nursery slopes of your career or because you have fallen down the rankings, and that probably means that you are struggling to make ends meet, so no five-star hotel for you. Oh no. Instead it would be a bed-and-breakfast establishment, where you hope and pray that they have changed the sheets, where the black-and-white television would only receive three channels (one of those in Welsh) and where you'd wonder if you could bring yourself to eat that fried breakfast, the one swimming in fat. Such were my experiences in the Prestatyn of the early 1990s. Glamorous? Hardly. But when you are starting out, as I was, Prestatyn and places like it are all part of the adventure.

'OK, Graeme, I've got a little bit of money,' said Uncle George. 'I think it is about time we headed off to Pontin's in Prestatyn and then we will find out how good you really are.' Pontin's at Prestatyn staged both a spring and an autumn festival. George took me to the spring festival in 1992 and I lost in the juniors to Paul Hunter in the semi-finals, but in the full tournament I got through to the last 32. Not bad going as I was only 14 at the time and even managed to beat Jimmy Michie, who was a professional player.

How did these men react to losing to a kid? Let's just say that they were not best pleased. At that time, when the tournament reached the last-32 stage, the field was augmented by a number of invited professionals – guys such as Mike Hallett and Tony Knowles. I was praying that I would be drawn against one of them but ended up facing Drew Henry, a fellow Scot. No disrespect to Drew but I could have played him any time in one of the pro-ams back home. I was going to lose anyway and I would rather it had been against the likes of Hallett or Knowles, but it wasn't to be. He duly beat me 4-0. In fairness, he was in a different league to me. And a few weeks later, when I was aged just 15, I also travelled with him to Pontin's in Hemsby, Norfolk, where the British Under-15 Championship was being staged. After an endless train journey we arrived, dumped our luggage in our chalet and went to register for the tournament, only to be told that I was too old.

'What?' I was devastated. 'We have spent all this time and money to get here from Glasgow and you are telling me that I can't play?'

'I am sorry but the rules are clear. You have to be *under* fifteen and you are not, but you can play in the Under-nineteen tournament if you want.'

We hadn't come all this way to turn round and go straight back home so I agreed to play, although I didn't think that I had a prayer. I told George what I had agreed but he has always been a man to seek out the positives, and his reaction was that I should do my best and see what happened. And what happened was that, incredibly, I ended up winning the Under-19 tournament, along with a cheque for £500. For the first time in my life, I truly began to realise how good a player I could become. My mind was made up: if I could win the British Under-19 Championship at the age of 15, I was going to try to make a living playing snooker.

Incidentally, you might have heard of the Welsh boy who won the Under-15 tournament. His name was Matthew Stevens. I often wonder what the outcome would have been if I had been allowed to compete in the same tournament. A promising Yorkshire teenager called Paul Hunter was also in the field.

By now, with Edinburgh-born Stephen Hendry dominating the professional game, there was a huge explosion of interest in snooker north of the border. Hailing from Hamilton, Jamie Burnett's career was starting to take off, as was that of Alan McManus, and not far behind was John Higgins. And I wanted to be part of it. I was trying to fit my snooker around my schooling so I wasn't able to spend as much time on the practice table as I would have wanted to. The good thing was that I was now winning pro-ams on a regular basis, which meant that I was just about able to pay my own way, which meant a lot to me.

If I wished, I could play in pro-ams on Sundays, Mondays, Wednesdays and Fridays, although the matches could drag on till midnight so, rather than play the final, myself and the other finalist would usually agree to split the money between us. At one point it seemed as if every time I played in a pro-am, I would either win it or reach the final. Consequently, I was suddenly starting to rake in the money and, for a boy who had never been used to having much more than bus fares in his pocket, this was an unbelievable experience.

CHAPTER THREE

THE MAN WHO CHANGED MY LIFE

Not long after my experiences at Pontin's, a man called Alex Lambie took a starring role in my life and things would never be quite the same again. A successful businessman in Larkhall who owned a hotel and bar called Berries, as well as a snooker club, Alex had a snooker-playing son of his own, also called Alex who, like me, participated in the junior tournaments at Reardon's. Alex Junior and I quickly became friends.

George felt that he had taken me as far as he could and he asked Alex if he would be interested in managing me. Alex had no experience either as a player manager or agent but George saw something in him and he obviously knew that Alex had some money – he was one of the first people in Larkhall to own a mobile phone, he always had good cars and he took his family on expensive foreign holidays.

When I returned to Prestatyn for the autumn festival, Alex was with me and this time I did really well, reaching the final of the main tournament. I beat some really good players, including three invited players, Hallett, Knowles and Les Dodd. But I lost to Wayne Brown in the final. Brown beat Neal Foulds in the other semi-final and I remain convinced to this day that, had I played Foulds in the final, I would have won.

You will remember that I told you about the handicap system. All the professionals (Hallett, Knowles, Dodd) had agreed to give me a 14 start although, when I knocked in a century break in my first frame against Dodd, he said with tongue firmly in cheek, 'This is a disgrace, me giving this boy a fourteen start. I should be giving him a lot more than fourteen.'

I played Mike Hallett in the quarter-final and Alex was sitting in the crowd when he overheard a conversation between two English spectators. 'This young Scottish kid is meant to be good but Mike will slaughter him,' said one of them.

Alex turned round. 'Do you think so? Would you like to have a bet on the outcome?'

That's the way he was. He would have seen me give Ronnie O'Sullivan a 20 start and still bet on me. It made me feel ten feet tall to know I had that level of support.

He had waved a pile of money in their faces but the English spectators backed down. It was just as well, as I beat Hallett 4-0. Alex took great delight in walking past the English pair at the end of the match and he enjoyed telling me the story afterwards. I don't suppose it helped my opponents when they took a good look at me – I was so skinny that, if I stood behind my snooker cue, I could just about disappear and they must have hated losing to such a player. I looked like a refugee. Even throughout my 20s I weighed only about 8 stone.

So how can I describe Alex Lambie? He was a big bear of a man who did not suffer fools gladly but, if he took to you, you had a loyal friend for life and a man who would do anything for you. His son Alex Junior was a good friend, and he also had a daughter called Elaine who was a few years younger than me. They were a great supportive family, who welcomed me into their fold yet asked for nothing in return.

In 1993, at the age of 16, I won the Scottish Amateur Championship in the exhibition suite at the Masters Club in Glasgow. I felt that I had arrived. Stephen Hendry had been the only man to be younger than me when he won it and, suddenly, I found myself being compared with him. What a buzz that was, I can tell you.

I played a guy called Neil Martin in the final and there was a row about his participation because he was a professional snooker player who had competed on the circuit and had gone straight from there onto the Scottish amateur scene. People thought it unfair, arguing that he should have waited a full year before playing amateur snooker again. I was incredibly nervous before the Martin match, and remember trying to play a few practice frames and being unable to pot a ball. The exhibition suite at the Masters only holds about a hundred people but it is a very enclosed area and you feel that they are right on top of you. I had played in front of a bigger crowd than this at Hemsby but that was not as claustrophobic as this was. It didn't help that almost every member of my family was in the crowd, but I somehow managed to concentrate on the match. Winning that encounter, and indeed the whole Scottish Amateur Championship, was a great feeling and, when the press told me I was second only to Hendry, I felt like I was walking on air.

After my victory, Alex agreed to become my manager, although I never really considered him to be one, at least not officially. We never drew up a contract and I don't think there was ever even much of a verbal agreement. It all just sort of happened, with Alex saying that he would sponsor me. In effect, he gave me a small weekly wage that covered my bus fares from my home in Dennistoun to Larkhall, where I could use his snooker club to practise every day. He paid my entry fees to tournaments, he covered the cost of petrol and he paid for the accommodation when we had to stay anywhere.

I agreed to give him 40 per cent of whatever I earned. There will be some people who might regard that as a lot but they have to remember that I was earning nothing and, however, you look at it, 40 per cent of nothing is still nothing. Ultimately, I would become like another son to Alex. He was like a father and a best friend to me. I'm sure he would much rather have offered this treatment to his own son but, although Alex Junior was a good enough player to turn professional himself, he would be the first to admit that he was never quite good enough to succeed at the very highest level. At least he could say that he gave it his best shot though and he was not merely a good practice partner for me but a great mate too. With a need to practice at least four hours a day at the Lambie house, and with Alex Junior as a close friend, I would often end up staying the night in Larkhall.

As soon as I could, I left school. Having won the Scottish Amateur I had decided that I was going to turn professional and now I had Alex to support me. If I told him that there was a tournament I wanted to play in, he would sort everything out, from entrance fees to travel to accommodation. The only thing I had to worry about was turning up and making sure that I was on top form.

After all the struggles, it is difficult to explain the sense of relief at not having to worry about every penny. Alex loved snooker and that helped, and we had an especially great time together whenever he accompanied me. Eventually he told me that I was going to have to buy myself a car. It was no good me having to get the bus here, there and everywhere. Nobody in my family could drive and, although Alex had been giving me driving lessons, I knew nothing about cars. No matter how hard I tried, I couldn't get my head round the concept of changing gears using a clutch. I was never able to get on with the gearstick and was about to throw in the towel when he suggested that I learn to drive in an automatic. And so it was that I passed my test in an automatic and that is all I have ever driven. Armed with a licence, I went out looking for a Vauxhall Corsa and ended up coming home in a BMW Compact – and I loved it.

After I had taken the decision to turn professional, little seemed to change for a time. Nowadays just about every player sports sponsors' logos on their waistcoats but it never entered our heads back then that there might be sponsors out there who would be prepared to part with their cash in order to be associated with Graeme Dott, snooker player. It just wasn't an option.

No, the thing to do was to go and play in tournaments and win lots of prize money, except that it isn't as simple as that. When you turn pro you are given a ranking based on what you have achieved as an amateur but you are still starting on the bottom rung of the ladder. Every new professional has to enter the qualifying tournaments and, if you don't win matches there, you might as well pack your suitcase, break your cue in two, throw it away and go find another career. If you can't break out of the qualifiers, you will not make a living playing snooker and your Careers teacher will be able to say, 'I told you so.'

I was determined that wasn't going to happen to me but I am not sure that I was fully aware of the size of the task facing me. Did I understand how difficult it was going to be? And if I had realised how soul-destroying it can be, would I still have done it? Of course I would have.

Does any sportsman at the beginning of a career consider the possibility of failure? I would imagine that the only ones who do are the ones who do fail. Self-belief is key and, thanks to the support of Alex Lambie and Uncle George, I had that in spades. As you will discover, it wouldn't always be that way but at the start of the journey there were no doubts in my mind that I could set targets for myself and then achieve them.

First and foremost, every snooker player wants to make it into the fabled top 16. Why? If the sport recognises you as one of the best 16 players, it means you do not have to pre-qualify for any tournament. It also means you get an invitation to The Masters at Wembley, you may be asked to play in the Premier League on Sky TV and you can go straight to The Crucible for the World Championships. You are also guaranteed to get plenty of television exposure, so you build a fanbase and become attractive to potential sponsors. Although there are not as many tournaments now as there were during snooker's golden days, if you remain in the top 16 for a number of years, you can be pretty sure that you will be making a decent living. For me and Alex, though, all of this was new.

The last tournament I played in before turning pro was the World Amateur in Pakistan, which was also the first time I had been abroad to play the game. We stayed in a marvellous five-star hotel in Karachi but the moment you stepped outside, the reality of life in Pakistan hit you right between the eyes. The streets were full of beggars, mostly young children, some without limbs. Poverty also has its own stench and it was sometimes difficult not to feel as though you were about to vomit. I lost in the semi-finals to Ron Surin but, had I been beaten in the first round, I would not have been too unhappy because it would have meant that we were able to leave for home. I couldn't get out of the place fast enough. I vowed that I would never return and I haven't.

Pichit was one of a number of players from Thailand who took part in that tournament and, by and large, they were in a different class to the guys from the West, including yours truly. If ever I doubted my ability in snooker, it occurred while I was watching those players. I later took consolation from the fact that, although they were amateur in name, they lived snooker morning, noon and night.

I also failed to take into account the fact that I was still only 16 years of age and I was bound to improve, whereas many of the Thai players were in their late 20s and had already reached their prime. George and Alex would constantly remind me how young I was and how much I still had to learn.

CHAPTER FOUR

PLAYING WITH THE BIG BOYS

S nooker was open, so anybody could turn pro. All that you had to do was pay your money to the governing body, which at the time was the World Professional Billiards and Snooker Association (WPBSA), and you could then play. The result was that something like 700 hopefuls would turn up at Blackpool's Norbreck Castle Hotel every summer for the qualifying competitions that seemed to go on for ever. It was a big hotel and the snooker hall was highly impressive. There were 10 practice tables and a further 22 tables in cubicles in the arena. Spectators? Don't be daft. I remember once that there might have been a man and his dog watching me.

I loved those early days because I was having the time of my life, although I couldn't sleep on the eve of my first match because I was so excited. My first opponent was a guy called Richard Batty and I beat him 5-0. It was the perfect start and I was thrilled to bits but, to give you a sense of the task that faced us, we would sometimes have to win as many as ten matches just to reach the knockout stages of a tournament. The one thing it did do was to get you match ready. I can promise you that any snooker player who came through all those qualifying rounds was ready to win when he arrived at the venue for the tournament proper, and that is precisely why there are always so many so-called surprise results.

There may have been a time when the top 16 players took some of the qualifiers for granted, assuming they were in for an easy match, but it didn't take long for that attitude to change. Let's say a player only qualifies for the final stages of one tournament. Don't you think that he is going to try to do whatever it takes to win a few matches when he gets there?

Not so very long ago, the unknowns might have struggled at the thought of playing in front of big crowds, under the TV lights, with the likes of Willie Thorne, Clive Everton and John Virgo passing judgement on every shot they play. Not now. When they get there, they are ready.

And so was I. But first of all there was the small matter of getting there. Alex paid all my entry fees, which came to about £2,000 before I had potted a ball. I wanted to start winning because I wanted to give Alex some money back. It didn't matter to him but it did to me.

The thought of going through endless qualifying matches now fills me with horror but it was an adventure back then. I would spend months on end in Blackpool and couldn't quite believe my luck. I was fortunate in that Alex had managed to find a great B&B, run by a couple called Jean and Geoff, and they became a bit like surrogate parents. With many guesthouse owners, you get the impression that they feel they are doing you a favour, so it was a joy to discover that Jean and Geoff really cared about the people who stayed under their roof. I received a letter not so long ago from Jean to tell me that her husband had died and I was genuinely sorry to hear the news. He was a lovely man.

One of the other things I loved about Blackpool was that for large parts of the summer it seemed that half the population were Scots who had arrived for their annual two-week holiday, so it was like a home from home for me when I did emerge into the daylight.

How did the qualifiers work? Let's say that the first set of qualifying matches was for the Grand Prix, so I would play my first-round match on the Monday and, if I won, I would probably play my second-round match the next day but, as you progress, you face better players because everybody is seeded. In those days, round one would normally be a formality because I would find myself facing somebody who had been a professional for ages but, to be frank, was rubbish. You would expect to win those games with one hand tied behind your back, but it quickly became more of a challenge.

By the time Thursday came along, I could be playing a fourth-round match and, if I won, that tournament would then effectively be frozen. On Friday, the first qualifying round for another tournament would begin – say the UK Open – and I would have to repeat the process all over again.

I was playing so much competitive snooker that I frequently lost track of who I was meant to be playing next and in what tournament. We would all gather in the practice area and Anne Yates, the tournament director, would arrive and give each of us our start time and the name of the player we were facing. Then we would leave the room and maybe start chatting with a fellow player, who would ask, 'Who are you playing today, Graeme?' Frequently my mind would just go blank and I would have to reply, 'You know what? I haven't the foggiest idea, I really haven't.' You would think that was impossible, but I am sure that I wasn't the only one.

There was a time one summer when I won a match and returned with Alex to the B&B, where we had a bite to eat before he left to go back to Glasgow. It was about 6pm and he was going home for the night then driving back the following day for my next match, which started at 10am the following day. I was shattered so I decided that I would go to bed and close my eyes.

We had a television in the room so the plan was to switch it on and perhaps take a quick nap but, as soon as my head hit the pillow, I was out like a light. I woke up with a start and looked at my watch. Oh my God, I've slept in, I thought. I jumped out of bed, got washed as quickly as I could and put on my suit, flew out of the B&B and raced towards the Norbreck Castle. Suddenly it dawned on me that all was not quite as it should have been. This was the middle of summer, so why was it dark at 9.30am? It was actually 9.30pm and I hadn't slept in at all.

I must admit that I do actually have some form on this front, having been docked a frame at the World Amateur Championship for missing my start time after sleeping in. I was determined that it wasn't going to happen again, although you will discover that, some years later, I managed to repeat the feat in spectacular fashion.

It didn't happen very often but, if I lost a first-round qualifying match, it would mean that I would be left kicking my heels for four or five days. Occasionally, instead of staying in Blackpool I would return to Glasgow for a few days, but that was unusual.

This process would be repeated for all nine ranking tournaments and at the end of it even I have to admit that, as much as I loved the town of Blackpool and the prospect of playing all those snooker matches, I was ready to come home.

We all stayed in bed-and-breakfast accommodation – some of us even stayed in the same guesthouses. Through it all we become a pretty close-knit group. I remember that, on one particularly hot summer's day, I looked out the window and saw a large group of my fellow players on the pavement outside, and I wondered what on earth they were all up to.

One of the players, a boy by the name of Matt Wilson, fancied himself as a bit of a runner and he was challenging the other players to a race around the block for £20 a go, which was a decent amount of money back then. In those days, before I became a lazy so-and-so, I quite fancied myself as a bit of a sprinter. I felt certain that I could beat him but I wanted to make sure there was no way that I could lose. I mingled with the other guys, standing back from the action and eventually Wilson asked if I wanted to take him on.

'I'm not very good at running – never have been. I am just not that fast,' I said.

'Don't worry. I will give you a start,' he replied. Gotcha! I couldn't believe my ears but I didn't want to agree too quickly.

'Well, I'd need a big start. Seriously, I am not very good. I may as well just hand over the twenty pound. You would slaughter me.'

He gave a head start to the end of the road, and I figured

that I could just about walk and still beat him. I won by a mile and he ended up handing over the money but he wasn't happy and told me he wanted to race me again, this time off level. And I beat him again. The other guys had been having side bets as well and I had told them that I was an absolute certainty to beat him, so a lot of them made money on me too.

On another occasion, I got locked out of the B&B. I had played in a match and headed back to the digs to tell them that I had won, then returned to the Norbreck Castle Hotel to watch some more snooker. When I got back the front door was locked and I realised that I'd left my key in my room. I didn't want to wake Jean and Geoff.

I could see that my room window was slightly ajar and I told Alex Junior, who was staying with me, that I was certain I could get in. He told me not to attempt it but I shimmied up the drainpipe and, as I was halfway up, I suddenly realised that if I fell I would probably kill myself. It was just as well it was young Alex at the foot of the drainpipe and not his father. I managed to get to the top and then clambered over onto the window ledge of somebody else's room. As I was reaching over to try to force open my window, Alex Junior was shouting from below, 'For God's sake, watch what you're doing. Watch what you're doing.' I was trying not to attract attention to myself but his shouting gave me the fright of my life, so much so that I nearly fell off the ledge. Somehow, I managed to get my window open and get into the room, then went downstairs to let Alex Junior in. I can't quite believe I did that but I am convinced that it was down to my naturally competitive spirit. It would, perhaps, have been easier to knock on the front door and just apologise for being late but climbing up the drainpipe was more of a challenge.

After my first time at Blackpool I had qualified for the knockout stages of three tournaments, which was an achievement of which I was very proud. I made it to Dubai and had to win nine matches to do it, including Steve Newbury, former world champion Joe Johnson and Neal Foulds. I phoned my Dad and told him, 'It was brilliant. I was playing on the practice table and you'll never guess what: Gary Wilkinson was on the next table and Neal Foulds was next to him.' I wasn't star struck but this was the world I was now inhabiting and when I saw these guys I thought to myself, I've made it. I am a proper player and I can beat these guys.

At the time, the late Alex Higgins was still playing, still trying to scratch a living, and still trying to get back into the big time. You never knew what you were going to get with the Hurricane. One day he could be as nice as pie, the next he could be a total sod. Higgins was a Protestant and he got involved in a discussion with Alex Lambie about religion. For some reason, Higgins had got it into his head that Alex was a Catholic, but he wasn't – he was a Protestant, just like Higgins.

Higgins was nipping away at Alex, which was not a good idea. Alex was a big brute of a man and he could handle himself, so much so that I recall seeing him breaking up a fight at Berries and he had two drunks hanging off him but he was still walking around. So Higgins was definitely picking on the wrong guy and eventually he said the wrong thing, so Alex got hold of Higgins' hand and squeezed the life out of it as he explained to him that he wasn't a Catholic. For the next four weeks or so, Higgins sported a bandage on his hand. Alex Lambie was not a man to be messed with although, in all the years I knew him, the two of us never exchanged a cross word.

Alex was incredibly superstitious. Before we would leave the B&B, I would always get my bowtie and waistcoat on and I was ready to go. As we would get in the car to drive to the hotel, he would always have a Pink Floyd song called 'Brain Damage' on the car's CD player. It was another key part of the routine. That song had to be played on the way to every single match. It lasted for 4 minutes and, after 1 minute and 33 seconds of the track, one of the band members laughed in the background. Alex actually timed it. We would leave the digs, expecting to pull up at the hotel just as the laughter was heard. If he got there too quickly, he would hold traffic up – anything so that the laugh happened at the right time. And on one of the rare occasions when he didn't get the timing right and I lost the match that day, he took responsibility. 'That was my fault,' he said, even though it had been me who was holding the cue.

Alex did some amazing things to help me. The more I played professionally, the more I was becoming aware of the differences that I needed to get used to. Chief among them was the table lighting. In a normal snooker hall the lights are not terribly bright but playing in competitions, especially on TV, it is like playing in bright sunlight. I had a regular table that I used at Alex's club in Larkhall and one day I happened to mention the lighting. I hadn't brought up the subject because I wanted him to do anything about; it was just a conversation we were having.

'Don't you worry about that, son. I will sort that out for you,' he said. 'No bother.'

'I don't want you to, Alex. Apart from anything else, those competition lights are really expensive.'

'Just you leave it to me.'

I didn't think any more about it.

The next thing I knew was that Alex appeared in Blackpool with a van and came staggering out carrying a competition-standard light. I walked into the club in Larkhall a couple of days later and there it was, already installed. 'You see, I told you I would get you a light.'

I spent much of the time in Blackpool on my own. Alex had a business to run back in Larkhall, although he would always manage to get back down to watch my matches. I hate to think how many miles he must have driven on account of me.

Flying out to the Dubai Classic in the autumn of 1994 was pretty special because all the players were on the plane. Alex and I sat next to each other and, as we looked around, we realised that we were sharing our flight with the likes of Steve Davis, Jimmy White and Stephen Hendry. It was all surreal to me. We arrived in Dubai and everybody was invited to attend the official opening ceremony. They do things properly in Dubai. I have never been one to have sporting heroes but White was my favourite player and I was standing with Alex, sipping a Coca-Cola, when I saw Jimmy walking towards us. My first instinct was to turn round and see who was behind me but there was nobody there. He came up to me with his hand outstretched and said, 'Hello, Graeme, I am pleased to meet you. I've heard a lot about you. I'm Jimmy.'

There may be some people who are happy to criticise Jimmy White and it is probably true that he did make mistakes and that he did not win as often as he should have done with his outrageous natural talent, but I thought he showed a touch of class that day and he helped to make me feel very welcome. He didn't need to do it. I was just amazed that he knew who I was. He was the only one.

I lost 5-2 to Ken Doherty in the first round of the Dubai Classic. There is nothing much else to say about it really – I played all right but nowhere near my best and certainly not well enough to trouble Doherty. But at least I'd got my first 'proper' match out of the way and picked up some useful ranking points.

I also qualified to play in the International Open the week after the The Masters at Bournemouth in February 1995, where I would face Ronnie O'Sullivan for the first time. We drove to the venue but stopped off at Wembley on the way to see John Higgins play O'Sullivan in the final of The Masters. O'Sullivan easily beat Higgins and I could not believe the atmosphere. We get used to playing snooker in a hushed environment but Ronnie was the local boy and the crowd were constantly calling out between shots. Although he never said anything, I am certain that Alex wanted me to sample the atmosphere as a spectator so that it would be easier for me to handle if I ever had to face anything like it as a player. He was convinced I would soon be playing in The Masters.

Wembley Arena is an amazing venue but it is not one of my favourites. Although the fans make a lot of noise, they are too far away from the table for my liking. I much prefer The Crucible in Sheffield, where you almost feel that you could reach out and touch the spectators. It is more intimate and most of the players prefer it.

The match against Ronnie at Bournemouth was one of the

featured games on television. The night before, Alex and I were in our hotel watching the snooker when they announced that O'Sullivan vs Dott would be shown live the following day. I felt sick to the pit of my stomach. This was another new experience.

'This is it, Graeme,' Alex said. 'This is us in the big time.' I couldn't sleep that night and, when I got up the next morning, I was back and forwards to the toilet. I was a bag of nerves and felt terrible. Not only was I going to be on TV but I was going to be playing Ronnie O'Sullivan.

Even though I went on to lose 5-3 to Ronnie, I showed to both him and the public that I could certainly play, unlike some players who collapse in a heap when they play on TV. I actually had a chance to level the match at 4-4 in the eighth frame, but narrowly failed to take it. Afterwards, Ronnie said in an interview that I was a very good player, that I had given him a tough match and that I was definitely one to watch for the future. That made me feel special.

I went on to finish my first season as a professional with an official ranking that put me something like 230th in the world, which wasn't bad for starters. Matthew Stevens and Paul Hunter had similar rankings.

When I wasn't playing in qualifiers or tournaments I was practising my snooker, usually with Alex Junior. Our only distraction would be the trip to what was then the video shop to rent a video, which we would sometimes watch in the evening if we weren't back in the snooker hall, or which would be saved as a special treat for when we came home.

I lived a pretty boring existence then and, to be honest, I still do. I don't smoke and I don't drink – alcohol seems to act like a poison to me. I don't like the taste of the stuff and whenever I have tried it I have felt ill. I can assure you that there are no sinister undertones to any of this; I am teetotal because my body has taken that decision.

That is not to say that I don't have any vices. For instance, open my fridge any time and you will find that it is full of cans of Irn Bru. 'Made in Scotland, from girders,' says the advertising slogan, but the reality, I am sure, is that it contains rather a high level of sugar. I dread to think what it does to both my teeth and my body but I own up to buying it in bulk. At least I can console myself with the knowledge that I am doing my small part for the Scottish economy.

Later in my career, I would discover that going abroad was a nightmare for me when it came to food. The worst was China, where I simply couldn't handle the local cuisine. Nowadays, Stephen Maguire and John Higgins make a joke of it and will often order for me because they know what I am going to eat. During the day, it will be a club sandwich, at night it will be a club sandwich and, if I want anything in my room, it will be… yes, that's right. I will not eat seafood either and the menus in the hotels in China tend to feature plenty of seafood and vegetables.

Wherever else we go, it always tends to be burger and chips. I will eat Chinese and Indian food at home, just as long as there are no vegetables in it. I don't eat vegetables, although I can just about cope with potatoes and, while I enjoy the taste of fruit, I don't eat much of it. Just talking about all this makes me realise how unhealthy my diet probably is, but it's what I like. I know that when I go to somewhere like China I really should try the local food but I can't face it. There's no justification for it – I could tell you it's because I don't know what I am eating but when I eat a burger I can't put my hand on my heart and say that I know what's in that either.

1995 marked the start of my second season as a professional and it began with another stint in Blackpool, only this time I didn't have to take part in so many qualifying matches because I started the year with some ranking points. To be honest, it was another year of consolidation but, as it turned out, I had more than enough to be getting on with elsewhere in my life.

The first signs of a health scare appeared while I was competing at Prestatyn. It is difficult to put my finger on how I first felt unwell but the chalets tended to be quite damp so I blamed it on that. Then I was playing in a match at Blackpool and I was really struggling, so much so that Alex took me to one side and asked what was wrong. I brushed it off and told him I was fine but then I found myself on the wrong end of a thrashing by Steve James and I knew that something wasn't right.

I was still living with Mum at the time and when I got home I immediately took to my bed, but I wasn't unduly concerned because I was fairly convinced that I had either a very bad cold or a dose of the flu. I had no appetite and then I started being sick constantly, until it reached the point where there was nothing left to bring up. I told Mum I felt awful and that I felt it was probably about time that she phoned a doctor, who came to the house, examined me and announced that I would be fine. But I was not fine and the following day Mum phoned the emergency doctor, who examined me, then went out into the hall to phone for an ambulance. She didn't know that I could hear her but I remember her words clearly: 'I need an ambulance. It's a blue light job but don't put it on.' In other words, it was an emergency but she didn't want me to know – except for the fact that I now did know. Hearing that call didn't do much for my wellbeing and I was in a panic.

I was taken to the Royal Hospital in Glasgow and, no matter how hard I tried, I couldn't speak. The pain in my chest was dreadful. The whole thing was a blur to me, although I can tell you that my parents feared the worst. Initially they thought I had a blood clot on my lungs but eventually they diagnosed me as suffering from pneumonia and pleurisy. It was a shock, to put it mildly. This was not supposed to happen to teenagers – and remember that I lived a mostly fairly healthy lifestyle. I didn't drink or smoke and I didn't abuse my body.

After a while I began to feel better, then George remembered that with membership of the World Snooker Association (WSA) came private health cover. I had been in the Royal for about a week before I was moved to the Nuffield Hospital in Glasgow. By now I was improving and a doctor at the Nuffield told me, 'Don't worry about anything, Graeme. You are basically here for a rest. We have everything under control and you will be here for about four or five days, then you can go home and get on with your life.' It was exactly what I wanted to hear and it also helped that the surroundings were rather more acceptable than those at the Royal, which is a great hospital but, when all is said and done, it is an NHS hospital.

Then I suffered a relapse and ended up feeling worse than ever. I was constantly in pain and my main memory is of ringing the bell and asking the nurse for painkillers, only to be told that I had been given as many painkillers as they could safely administer. The pain in my chest was indescribable and they kept giving me heat pads to ease it, but nothing eased the pain.

At one point a doctor admitted to me that he hadn't a clue why I wasn't getting any better. I remember thinking, Well, if he doesn't know what's the matter with me, what chance have I got of coming through this?

They tried every possible combination of antibiotics, but nothing seemed to work. I later found out that Mum was leaving the hospital in tears most days, convinced that I was going to die. I used to lie in bed at night and wonder whether I would see the next morning. Eventually the drugs they were giving me started to work and I began to perk up. Fortunately, this time there was no relapse.

In all, I was ill for 3 weeks but they were the longest 21 days of my life and I also lost weight that I couldn't afford to lose. At that time, my fighting weight was around eight and a half stone, so losing any more weight just wasn't an option for me. In those days I could eat and eat and eat, and not put on any weight. Even now I only tip the scales at ten stone.

Recovered once more, I was able to concentrate on snooker again. The first game I played after I came out of hospital was against James Wattana in Bournemouth. He beat me 5-4 but I was just happy to be back in action. However, it was in January 1996, during the Regal Welsh Open at Newport, that I finally felt I had arrived in the big time. First of all I beat Dene O'Kane of New Zealand. Then I beat Alan McManus 5-4 in the second round and next up was John Higgins, who I beat for the first time by 5-4. It was a huge boost to my confidence, even though John Parrott beat me 5-2 in the quarter-finals. I thought, You have beaten two of the best players in the world here. You really do belong. Now let's see if we can kick on.

It is difficult to explain just how different the conditions are between qualifying events and tournaments. As I have already said, in a qualifier you basically play your match in a boxed-off cubicle with maybe ten spectators at the most and no TV lights. It is you, your opponent and a referee. When you reach the knockout stages of a tournament, suddenly you have to deal with the crowds, the television lights (which give off a tremendous amount of heat), TV cameras that follow your every move and games that are much faster paced. On top of that, when you first get there you will be playing guys who are better than you. If you make one mistake, the frame is gone, whereas you can drop the odd clanger in a qualifier in Blackpool and not be punished for it.

When you are consistently losing matches, I suppose it is only natural to think, I am never going to make it; these guys are just too good for me. What I didn't realise then was that I was learning as I was going along and, once I beat McManus and Higgins, my self-belief and confidence began to grow.

I couldn't tell you how much I was earning in those early seasons but it wouldn't have been much more than about £6,000 and it was costing Alex serious money to keep me on the circuit. But he never once complained or said that he wasn't prepared to continue. If anything, his belief in my ability became even more unshakable as the weeks turned into months.

I suppose that he also saw that Welsh Open tournament as something of a turning point. He could see the bigger picture. I wanted to be winning tournaments immediately and it took me a long time to work out that he was right when he said, 'It will come, Graeme. I know it will. You are improving. You are getting better and you will start beating these boys on a regular basis. You just have to be patient.' Every time I lost a match I was learning something, whether it was that I shouldn't have attempted a risky pot or that I should have played a safety shot at a given time.

I didn't even have a coach. When I was about 14 years old I won 4 free lessons from a Scottish coach called Eddie Gill and he ironed out the kinks in my action, teaching me to tuck in my elbow and stuff like that. I knew my own game inside out and knew what to look for if I started to miss easy balls. People look at players such as Jimmy White and Ronnie O'Sullivan and regard them as natural talents, and I have always regarded myself in the same way. I have always played snooker by instinct. There may be times when it hasn't looked that way but I can assure you that I have never been one to think about my cue action.

Although nothing spectacular was happening for me, I was making steady progress through the world rankings. I went from 190th to 58th to 33rd, then I squeezed into the all-important top 32 with a world ranking of 30 in 1999.

The pinnacle of any player's career is the World Championship and in our sport it is always played at The Crucible Theatre in Sheffield during late April and early May. My love affair with The Crucible had begun back when I qualified to play there for the first time in 1997, which was the year that Ken Doherty beat Stephen Hendry in the final, and when the Labour government came to power with Tony Blair as Prime Minister.

The first thing that struck me about The Crucible in real life was how small it was, with a seating capacity of just over 900 – on television it just looks so much bigger. And then there is that thing with the crowd, who seem to be so close to the action. The press box is situated just behind the table and you can look straight into the commentary box. There isn't another venue like it. You could move the Championship to Wembley and have three times as many people in the place but it wouldn't come close to reproducing the atmosphere or, crucially, the pressure we experience in Sheffield. If you can't get up for The Crucible, you should find something else to do for a living.

Don't get me wrong, it's not all perfect. If you take a potential sponsor backstage, he is probably going to ask himself, Is this it? Is this all there is? When I started playing there the players' dressing rooms were pretty shabby, with a wooden bench on which they had put a thin mattress, along with two chairs and a sink, but they have now been tidied up and are much, much better. The lounge is too small and it is hard to get all the television crews in but, from snooker's perspective, it is perfect. There has been talk in recent times about moving the World Championship to a bigger venue than The Crucible but I would resist such a change with every fibre of my being.

To secure my place in 1997 I defeated Belfast-born Joe Swail 10-8 in the final qualifying round. It was a great result because he was ranked 17th in the world at the time and had just

Above: Alex and May Lambie, both of whom died far too early.

Below: The best of friends – Jim Fisher has helped me through some of the toughest times in my life.

Above: Young boys together – with Alexander Lambie Jr at a junior tournament.

Below: Golden girls – my wife Elaine and my Mum after I won the World Championship

Above: Dad, Elaine and Alex share the proudest moment of my snooker career at Sheffield's Crucible Theatre.

© *Snookerimages*

Below: Elaine with her father shortly before he passed away.

That's my boy! Alex congratulates me after a junior victory.

bove: Berries, the pub Alex owned in Larkhall and where I was a member of the
ool team.

elow: The weather did its best to spoil our wedding day, but a local garden centre
me to the rescue.

Dressed to kill. Elaine and
on the happiest day of r
life – check out those le

above: Daddy's girl. Alex and Elaine on our wedding day.

below: A family affair. Elaine with her parents, May and Alex, at Berries.

Blue is the colou
Showing off the wor
championship troph
at Ibrox – they change
the colour of the ribbon
before allowing m
onto the pitc

missed out on getting into the tournament automatically. Nobody gave me a prayer but I came out on top and I couldn't wait to get to Sheffield. This was what it was all about; this was why I played this frustrating game.

In my first round match I faced James Wattana of Thailand, who was one of the best players in the world at the time. The first session was an overwhelming experience. Initially I took my seat, thinking, This is OK. I can handle this. And then the partition started to come down and I felt claustrophobic. 'Jeez, I'm not going to have any room to play. My cue is going to hit that wall. They must have made a mistake.' In reality, there was plenty of room but, for me, it was like the walls were closing in and, during that first session, I couldn't pot a ball. Somehow I finished it trailing just 6-3 and I did eventually get my act together when we returned to finish the match.

In the end Wattana beat me but I gave him the fright of his life and he only just won by a whisker: 10-9. Of course, you never like to lose a match but I was thrilled to have sampled the atmosphere. I had taken the conscious decision never to go to The Crucible before then because I wanted to experience it as a player. It was everything that I hoped it would be, and more besides. That defeat meant that I finished the year ranked 33rd in the world.

When the interval arrives in televised matches, the commentators will announce that the players are heading off to have a cup of tea, but I cannot think of a single player who does that. Most of us head back to the dressing room to gather our thoughts, or maybe pop into the players' lounge for a chat. There would be times when I would sit down in the dressing room with Alex and talk about the game but there were other times when I would prefer to talk about anything but.

Some players use those 15-minute intervals to go and hit a few balls but I have never been able to see the point in that. If you are struggling with your game, you are not going to put it right during an interval between sessions. I have this theory that, if you have been playing poorly and you go on to the practice table and start potting everything in sight, it would do your head in completely because you would end up asking yourself, Why the hell can't I do this out there, where it really matters? If it's meant to be your day, it will be your day.

The spectators at The Crucible are amazing, making you feel welcome right from the off and the city just buzzes during the two weeks that the tournament is played. It is all about the snooker and you can't go anywhere without being asked for your autograph, which has always made me feel rather special. When I was playing on my half-size table back in Easterhouse I never dreamed for a moment that somebody would walk up to me holding an autograph book and ask for my signature. You read stories about footballers and would-be pop stars who, in their teens, would endlessly practise their signature. Not me.

I didn't know it at the time but it would be a further three years after 1997 before I would return to the World Championship. In 1998 I lost 10-9 in the qualifiers to David Roe and the following year Marco Fu thrashed me 10-4 in the final qualifying round. So near yet so far – and it hurt like hell.

CHAPTER FIVE

THE LOVE OF MY LIFE

I have known Elaine Lambie for years. Obviously, she was always around when I spent time at Alex's house and she would sometimes hang out with Alex Junior and I, although she was four years younger than me. Initially I suppose that I regarded her as a little sister. She was certainly somebody that I cared about from quite early on.

I began to look upon her rather differently in 1998, when she was 16 years old. My feelings for her developed into something way beyond friendship and she felt the same way, but it was important to both of us that we did everything properly. I didn't want to sneak around behind her father's back but I was worried about how he would react.

Alex was a strict father; nobody was ever good enough for his daughter and he wouldn't let her go out with just anybody. I remember being in the house when boys would phone and ask to speak to her. If he answered, the person on the other end of the phone would soon regret making that call. 'Who is this?' he would demand. 'What do you want with Elaine? No, you can't talk to her and don't phone here again.' It was quite intimidating to hear him talk to boys that way and some of them were genuinely no more than friends. So I was worried about how he would react when he discovered that I wanted to start taking his daughter out. There was only one way to find out.

In the end, though, he was great about it. I suppose that, in his heart of hearts, he probably wanted the two of us to get together. I guess that he was relieved when I began to show an interest because he knew me as well as my own father did, and he knew that I wouldn't hurt Elaine. If I ever had done, I would have had Alex to answer to.

My parents were also delighted about our relationship. I was in the car with Mum one day and said to her, 'I've got something to tell you.' Before I could say anything else, she butted in, 'You and Elaine are going out.'

I went out and bought Elaine a Rennie Mackintosh gold ring, which she still has. She used to come with me to Blackpool in the early days of my career and, when I wasn't playing snooker, we would head off to the Pleasure Beach with Alex Junior in tow. They were great days. I tried to make her feel special whenever I could, even if it only meant getting her a card that said, 'I love you'.

We went out together for a few years and then, in 2000, decided to buy our first home: a house in Larkhall, for £70,000. It sounds like a pittance but I still worried about being able to afford the mortgage. I had always said that I wanted to buy a house before we got married because I wanted us to live together first, just to make sure that we really were meant to be together. Again, I wasn't too sure how Alex would respond to me living with his daughter out of wedlock but he was fine about that too. If it had been anybody else, his attitude might well have been somewhat different. In his eyes, his daughter was with somebody he regarded as being a good person; somebody who would not mistreat her. He was also confident that I would be able to provide for her. Elaine had also stayed with me at my Mum's on many occasions, so I knew that it was all going to work out.

In 2002 I decided to ask Elaine to marry me. I don't do grand romantic gestures; I had always told her that, when I did so, it would not be at the top of the Eiffel Tower or anything like that. So I decided to make her a meal. I should mention that I don't cook so, when I say that I made her a meal, what I mean is that I 'made' a microwave meal, although I did at least manage to do some vegetables to go with it.

When she arrived home, having been at college, she did a double take and assumed I was after something.

'Do you want to play golf tomorrow or something?' she said.

Why is it that women always think the worst?

'No, I just thought that I would do your dinner for you, that's all.'

She later told me that she knew I was building up to something but she just wasn't certain what it was. We are friendly with former snooker player Billy Snaddon and his wife Tracey, and some days earlier we had been with them and Elaine had admired Tracey's engagement ring. It perhaps wasn't the most subtle approach in the world but I eventually plucked up the courage to say, 'Why don't you phone Tracey and ask her where she got her engagement ring?'

Within five minutes Elaine had been on the phone to everybody she knew to tell them I had asked to marry her. She said yes, by the way. That conversation took place on a Friday. By the Monday Elaine had the church booked.

We were married on 27 June 2003. When we came out of the church, not only was there our own official wedding photographer, but there were lots of press photographers too. It rained non-stop – well, we did get married in Scotland, after all. But this was serious rain, battering down all day long. Our wedding photographs were supposed to be taken in the beautiful gardens of the hotel where our reception was being held, but the weather was so dreadful that it was impossible. In the end, the photographer took us to a garden centre. I had a kilt on and we were all dressed up to the nines, walking through this garden centre. I have often wondered what the customers must have thought. The photographer did a fantastic job and nobody would ever have known. Finally, in the evening, the sun finally came out, so everybody was able to venture outside. But our only real regret on our big day was that May, Elaine's mother, was not around for her daughter's wedding, having died the previous year.

The day after we got married, we went to the airport to fly off on our honeymoon to Mauritius. While we were waiting for our flight, we bought a copy of the *Daily Record* and there we were inside it. That was when the occasion really hit us both. DOTT TIES THE KNOT said the headline. Really original, eh?

Elaine and I were sharing our home life with two Labradors, Sash and Buster. They were wonderful dogs. Lots of you will understand exactly what I mean when I say that they were our kids before we had children. They went everywhere with us and we loved them. Sash arrived first and we doted on him. Then, after one of my friends had a bitch and decided to breed from it, we fell in love with Buster. In fact, I bought Buster without telling Elaine that I intended to do so. She was out of the house when I went to collect him and when I got back I put a blue ribbon on him and popped him in the bath. On Elaine's return I told her that I thought there was something wrong with the bath and that I couldn't get it clean. She was thrilled when she saw Buster.

Occasionally there was a minor domestic drama to deal with. One night Elaine was at home and I was out walking Sash when I bumped into a neighbour, who told me that there had been reports of a prowler in the area. Apparently he had been trying to break into a couple of houses. This was at about 11.30pm so when I came home I told Elaine and we made sure that all the doors were locked before we headed to bed. We have blinds in our bedroom and when they are closed the room is pitch black. I remember thinking about the prowler before I nodded off to sleep and I woke with a start when I heard a noise. It sounded like somebody was trying to force open the front door but then it went quiet so I tried to go back to sleep. I heard another noise and then what sounded like a bang. I was starting to panic, then I heard footsteps coming up the stairs.

I shook Elaine to wake her up.

'There's somebody in the house. There's somebody in the house.'

We have an en suite so I told her that we would have to go in there and phone the police. By now Elaine was also in a panic. She grabbed the phone and rushed into the bathroom, and I followed her in and closed the door. But still the footsteps kept coming. Did I mention that both of us were starkers?

'Elaine, phone the police and tell them we've got intruders in the house. Quickly.'

As she got through to the police station, I opened the bathroom window to shout for help and, as I did so I, found myself staring right into the window cleaner's eyes!

I tried to remain nonchalant. 'All right, mate?' And then I gently closed the window and told Elaine, who by now had got through to the police, that we didn't have a burglar after all: the noise I had heard was the window cleaner setting up his ladders. Elaine had to apologise to the police, explaining it had been a misunderstanding: 'It's OK, officer. It's the window cleaner.'

Elaine and I got on like a house on fire right from the start and we still do. No matter what life has thrown at us – and it's thrown a lot – we stick together and face it. She is my rock and I could not imagine my life without her.

As well as being a brilliant mother to our two children, she is also a fully qualified regional general nurse. She works as an agency nurse but, obviously, it has to fit around my snooker. When I am at home I look after the children so that she can go to work. We are in a position where she doesn't have to work but she does it because she wants to, and because she feels that she can make a difference to people's lives. She has found her vocation and I am so proud of her; nursing is extremely gruelling and I could never do it.

Having worked so hard, Elaine more than deserves a summer holiday. I can take or leave lying in the sun and am happy enough with the glorious scenery of Scotland (despite the weather) but Elaine loves the sun, so every year she takes care of booking it all and we duly head off somewhere hot for a couple of weeks. The snooker season finishes early in May, so it means that I get quite a long break from then until August, during which we can get away from it all.

We usually get somebody to give us a lift to Glasgow airport because it means that I don't have to worry about parking the car and all the hassle that goes with it. On one occasion, when we had booked a scheduled flight to Spain, it was Alex who dropped us off at the terminal. When we got inside the terminal I checked the departure board and there was no mention of our flight. We weren't concerned because, as usual, we had arrived in plenty of time. But as time went by and there was still no sign of our flight on the departure board, we joined a queue. When we got to the front I explained how surprised we were that there was no sign of our flight. The woman looked at our tickets and said, 'I am not surprised there is no sign of your flight on the departure board. Today is the sixteenth of July. Your flight departed on the sixteenth of *June*.'

There wasn't much more to be said.

'Hello Alex. It's Graeme. You are not going to believe what's happened...'

CHAPTER SIX
STARRING PERFORMANCE 1998-99

*T*he professional doubts I'd been experiencing finally disappeared during the 1998 – 99 season. I sometimes think it would have happened sooner for me had I been English. There is something about the Scottish psyche that sees us enjoying playing the underdog. There are times when we almost revel in coming off second best but, by and large, you just don't find that attitude in England.

English sportsmen and women have a natural confidence; a swagger that sets them apart. I have no idea why that should be and I am equally certain that many people will think I am talking nonsense and will point to the likes of tennis's Andy Murray. I agree that Murray is a born winner and that he appears to have a kind of super-confidence but I am not convinced that it is natural and, if it is, he is clearly an exception to the rule.

As 1998 was drawing to a close I found myself suffering a crisis of confidence – the first real low point of my career so far. Alex knew that my head was not in a good place so he suggested that I go and spend some time with Terry Griffiths, the former world champion who had been establishing a great reputation as a coach. I got in touch with him and he invited me to come down to see him in Wales.

He watched me playing a few shots and saw nothing wrong with my technique. 'I don't want to change a thing about your game, Graeme, but I do think that we need to sit down and have a long chat about what is going on inside your head, because I am convinced that is where the root of your problems lie.'

We taped our four-hour conversation so that I could listen to it again whenever I felt the need. I still have the recordings and still listen to them from time to time. As I talked to the former world champion, I realised that all my difficulties were, as he'd suggested, in my head. For a start, I wasn't thinking or motivating myself properly. Griffiths also believed – and I agreed – that you should get yourself psyched up before a contest in much the same way as the world's best boxers do. But you cannot leave all this stuff until the last minute before a tournament.

During matches, I would miss shots and walk back to my seat in disgust but, rather than keeping my emotions to myself, I would carry on shaking my head, or would bury my head in my hands. These were tell-tale signs to my opponent that I was all over the place, which would end up boosting their confidence so his game would improve, and I would finish off feeling even more depressed. You should never show an opponent that you are bothered.

My attitude was wrong then but something clicked in my

mind during those hours with Griffiths. He asked me what my next tournament was and I told him it was in Scotland a couple of months later. 'Right then, Graeme,' he said. 'I want you to start preparing yourself mentally for that tournament right now. Don't wait until the night before you get there. Start thinking about it now: about the venue, about the tables, about the atmosphere you will face, about the players you will have to beat.'

That tournament was the Regal Scottish Open in Aberdeen, which was to take place a few months later in February 1999. My morale was helped by knowing that I would be playing in front of a Scottish crowd. With such an amazing atmosphere likely, I had no difficulty lifting my mood in anticipation and so, when the time came, I was ready – and then some.

I defeated Jimmy Michie 5-4 in the first round, Quentin Hann 5-2 in the second round and John Parrott 5-4 in a tight third-round match. Then I faced Paul Hunter in the quarter-final. He went 3-1 ahead and then led 4-2 but I dug deep and won the last three frames, clinching the decider with a break of 60.

So, I had reached my first ranking-tournament semi-final and came up against Ken Doherty, then in his prime. The venue was packed and I could not believe how passionate the crowd were. They were desperate for me to win that match and roared at every break, every successful frame. Doherty had experienced this sort of thing many times in his career but it was a whole new experience for me and I loved every single moment of it. There is no player who is more difficult to beat than the Irishman but, after a ding-dong battle, I won the last two frames to beat him 6-5.

At that time, it would have been enough of a buzz to reach any final of a tournament but to do it in my homeland was beyond my wildest dreams. My opponent was to be Stephen Hendry – for me the greatest player ever to draw breath – who had beaten John Higgins in the other semi-final. It was the best of 17 frames, played over 2 sessions, and I was overawed by it all. It was the first time I'd had to deal with all the pressures that go with having all your family and friends in the arena – I knew how badly they wanted to see me win and I suppose it meant some added pressure on my shoulders.

The journey to the final had been hard work and it was no great surprise that I found myself 8-0 down against Hendry before I knew where I was. It was also the first time in the tournament where I became aware that I wasn't the crowd favourite – he was. The standard of snooker wasn't great, with Hendry's biggest break being a 74. I made a 60 in the 7th frame but still lost it as he rolled in a 70. I did eventually get a frame on the board but lost 9-1, although I didn't play as badly as that score line might suggest because there were a lot of frames I could have won. The difference between us was that I would get in and make a 40-odd break and he would then come to the table and clear up.

As happy as I was to have reached my first final, I had been made painfully aware of just how much I still had to do because Hendry was on a different planet to me. I was embarrassed by the margin of defeat and I struggled to find the positives. When it was all over I also felt an overwhelming sense of sadness – not because I had lost but because the tournament was finished, and the incredible atmosphere and the buzz were gone. I went back to the venue and all the practice tables were gone. 'Is that it? Is that all there is?' It felt like I had been hit by a sledgehammer. But at least I could console myself with the knowledge that I had picked up a nice cheque for about £32,000, made a few headlines and earned a bucket-load of ranking points that would take me closer to my goal of getting into the top 16.

I was even approached by Ian Doyle, who managed Stephen Hendry through the best years of his career, who asked if he could look after me. He took me out for a nice meal to explain everything that he could do for me. I was upfront with Alex and told him that I had been approached and he said that he was happy for me to meet Doyle and would understand completely if I decided that I wanted to sign with him.

In the event, Alex came with me. I listened to everything that Doyle had to say. He told me that he would get me into the Regal Masters, which was a tournament he ran every September, and he said he could find me sponsors, but that was it. I don't know what I had been expecting but there was nothing on the table that I wasn't already getting or doing. Signing for him was never really a serious consideration. Alex had shown faith in me since the first time he had seen me play and there was no way that I was going to walk away from him. I slept on it, then told Alex I was staying with him, before phoning Ian Doyle with the words, 'Thanks but no thanks.'

I never did get an invitation to play in the Regal Masters, which I always thought was a bit strange. For a start, it was played at Motherwell, which is almost on my doorstep. And it seemed that every other Scottish player got a chance to play – Hendry, McManus, Higgins, Chris Small, Drew Henry, Billy

Snaddon. But not me. For a lot of matches there was never a big crowd but there would have been if I had been playing.

Because Alex was effectively sponsoring me, I had never really thought about the financial side of things back then. That has all changed now, of course, but my priorities were different back then. I'd rediscovered my appetite for the game.

CHAPTER SEVEN

MAXIMUM EXPOSURE 1999

I have never had any problems scoring decent breaks and have picked up the odd high break prize here and there, but I have never been the sort of player who is able to make maximum breaks of 147 for fun the way that the likes of Ronnie O'Sullivan and Stephen Hendry have been able to do throughout their careers, both in match play and on the practice table.

I had managed a few of my own away from the tournament scene but hadn't really come close to it when the chips were down. There are some players who start thinking about maximums after they have potted, say, four reds and four blacks, but my priority has always been to get the frame won and, if that means potting a simple pink rather than taking on a risky black, I will always go for the pink. To me, it is the right thing to do, especially if missing that black could mean that you lose the frame. Why would any player want to take that sort of risk?

Alex Junior was the guy who was usually on the wrong end of my maximum breaks in practice and I had also made a couple in pro-ams and amateur events but, of course, what you really want is to do it in a tournament, in front of a decent crowd and with the TV cameras in attendance.

I finally achieved that goal at the British Open in Plymouth on 6 April 1999, where my opponent was David Roe. I was trailing 4-3 at the time in that match so I had to win the frame to stay in the match. The thought of recording a maximum never once entered my head until I had scored about 56, with seven reds and seven blacks. I looked around the table and realised that the reds were situated pretty well so I decided to have a go at it.

The problem was that I had terrible problems staying in position and I ended up having to pot a series of great shots. In reality, it was probably the 'best worst' 147 break ever seen. When I got to the colours I had a horrible yellow but managed to get it in, although it left me with a really difficult shot on the green. I had to use the rest but, again, I potted it. Now the cue ball was situated in a straight line between the blue and the brown, leaving me with another fine cut on the brown and, again, I had to use the rest.

The brown disappeared but my position on the blue wasn't perfect and this time I was left with a difficult diagonal pot. Next was the pink, which was off its spot. I knew that all I had to do was play a stun run-through and I would be perfect for the black but I hit it all wrong and realised, to my horror, that I had left myself a possible in-off on the final ball of the break. I'd made 140, won the frame and knew that I had nothing to lose so I played the shot, the black rolled into the pocket and, in the event, the cue ball ran safe.

The venue at Plymouth was an unusual one in some ways. There were seats around the tables but there was also a balcony from where people could watch the snooker. I remember looking up at one point during my break and realising that everybody was watching me. Snooker fans are incredibly knowledgeable and they wanted to see a 147 break. As I got closer to it, the cheers grew louder and louder. What a feeling!

They say that the most difficult thing to do after recording a maximum is to win the next frame. But I had no choice, so I took myself out of the arena for a quick toilet break and gave myself a talking to: 'Right boy, all that you have done is to level the match. It means nothing unless you can get out there now and win the deciding frame.' And I did. It was such a pleasure to be able to share my victory with Alex and Alex Junior, who were in the crowd, and I am sure that they enjoyed it every bit as much as I did.

Life on the road is an odd existence but living out of a suitcase is part of what we do and that aspect of things really didn't bother me. When you get married and have children, of course, it becomes more difficult. I cannot imagine many things worse than coming home to be told that your son or daughter has said their first word or has taken their first step while you were gone.

At an average tournament there will be two or three practice tables and we are all allocated time on those tables through putting your name up on a sheet on a wall. All the players undertake these sessions on their own – you only have 30 minutes at a time, maybe an hour, and we use this time to get into a routine, to free up our arm and just get the feel for potting balls. I would have Alex with me and he would re-spot the balls for me.

I still hadn't cracked the top 16 but being ranked at 30 did, at least, mean that when I went back to Blackpool for the summer-1999 qualifiers, I only had to play one qualifying match in each tournament. Terry Griffiths had told me that it was important to set targets for myself and I did that at the start of each season.

No matter where you are ranked, the thing that drives you on is the desire to get better; to climb the rankings. The guy who is 701st in the world will regard it as progress to get to 700th, the guy who is 17th is desperate to get to 16th and the player who is 2nd in the world dreams of becoming No. 1. The most difficult thing of all is being ranked No. 1 and staying there, because everybody is gunning for you. And I do mean everybody.

I had come into the professional game alongside Matthew Stevens and Paul Hunter. Initially we all climbed the rankings at about the same rate of progress but Matthew and Paul left me behind after about three or four years. While I was struggling, they were flying, and I felt left out of things. I would switch on the television and there they would be, playing in the final stages of tournaments. I couldn't understand why they were there and I wasn't. There was nothing for it but to get my head down and work even harder.

I will return to Paul's career later on but, first, a little more on Matthew. During the 1997 – 98 season he reached the semi-finals of the Grand Prix and the UK Championship, as well as the quarter-finals of the World Championship, before finishing as runner-up to John Higgins the following season in the final of the UK Championship. By 2000 he had won the Benson and Hedges Championship, the Regal Scottish and The Masters, and he was riding high in the top 16. He also reached the final of the World Championship in 2000, losing 18-16 to Mark Williams in an excellent final. On top of that, as a team player, he had won the 1999 Nations Cup with his beloved Wales.

I knew that I was as good a player as Matthew was. Why wasn't I doing as well as him? It made no sense to me.

CHAPTER EIGHT

THE OLD FIRM
– 2000

I have tried to explain the rivalry between Rangers and Celtic to some of my fellow professional snooker players but they just don't get it. They do not comprehend the hatred that exists between the two sets of supporters.

I first went to Ibrox as a six-year-old with my father. I loved the atmosphere, and the passion and excitement when Rangers scored. If I am being honest, I probably also enjoyed all the singing and chanting but that was only because I didn't understand what any of it meant. Yes, the songs are sectarian, but the reason that the fans sing them is because they know the opposition don't like it, and the Celtic fans sing their songs because they know we don't like it. I believe the songs are banter and should be treated as such, and the attempts to make supporters stop singing them seem pretty fruitless to me.

Arsenal fans hate Tottenham fans and vice versa but you never hear anybody saying that the songs they sing against each other should be banned. They are part of the game; part of the culture of football. Some of the stuff that Leeds fans sing about Manchester United are a lot worse than what Rangers supporters sing about Celtic. Those Leeds fans are singing about the Munich disaster; about the deaths of innocent people in a plane crash.

The most terrifying experience of my life happened at the end of a Celtic–Rangers Old Firm match at Parkhead. It was 27 August 2000, Celtic had just beaten us 6-2 and I was devastated. To be fair, Celtic had been magnificent. They were 3-0 up after just 11 minutes thanks to goals from Chris Sutton, Stilian Petrov and Paul Lambert, and Henrik Larsson was pulling the strings. What a fantastic footballer he was. Claudio Reyna pulled one back before half-time but then Larsson scored a great goal and, although we scored from the penalty spot, Larsson and Sutton completed the scoring. It was a rout.

I had driven from Larkhall, left my car at Mum's and then made my way to the ground by taxi. I would never wear a Rangers scarf at Celtic Park. It is just asking for trouble. And I also worry about being recognised; I am a fairly high-profile sportsman in Scotland and, as such, everybody knows that I support Rangers but I refuse to let that stand in the way of me being able to watch my team.

The ground at Ibrox is designed in such a way that it is easy to keep rival fans apart and, at the end of all Old Firm games, the police keep the Celtic supporters in the ground until their rival fans have had a chance to disperse. It is different at Celtic Park, where the Rangers fans are allowed to congregate in two areas. But at the end of this particular match no attempt was made to keep the fans apart and mayhem ensued. Everywhere I looked there were Celtic fans and fights were breaking out all over the place. I had been at the match on my own and I just wanted to get home but that seemed a pretty unlikely prospect.

I got in among a group of Rangers supporters but the police were trying to shepherd us in exactly the opposite direction to the way I wanted to go, so I decided to break away from the group. Wearing no colours and keeping my head down, I was sure I would be fine, just as long as nobody recognised me.

There was a Rangers fan walking in front of me and, walking in the opposite direction, there was a Celtic supporter. As he reached the Rangers fan he punched him in the face and broke his nose. It was totally unprovoked. As I turned a corner a policeman told me that I couldn't go that way and the more I protested, the more determined he became. The last thing on earth I wanted was to get myself arrested.

As I looked round, I saw a group of about ten Rangers supporters walking along the road. Although they were wearing club colours, I figured that I was probably going to be better off with them; at least if any of the Celtic fans recognised me, I would have a bit of back-up if things turned nasty, so I fell in behind them. It was not a good move. These guys were singing Rangers songs and shouting and swearing, and it seemed to me that they were trying to do everything within their power to get themselves attacked.

Everywhere around us, grown men were fighting each other, while policemen on horses were riding into them and trying to break it up. It was like something out of a horror film. I had already made up my mind that I was never coming back to another match at Celtic Park. 'Please, just let me get out of this in one piece.'

There were only ten of us but still these idiots were singing and, the next thing we knew, coins were raining down upon us so we were walking along the road with our hands over our heads. Then these guys decided it would be a good idea to kick out at passing cars. It was as if they had some sort of death wish. I desperately wanted to tell them to shut up and to behave themselves but I was scared that they would turn on me.

With people now spitting at us, my only option was to take my chances and go it alone. As we reached the main street and I prepared to break away from them, we saw thousands of Celtic fans to the right of us and thousands more to the left of us, and they were walking towards us. I thought my number was up and I felt the colour draining from my cheeks but the guys I was with were loving it. Now they were singing UVF songs and shouting, 'Fuck the Pope.' With that, the Celtic fans started charging at us and I thought, That's it. I'm dead.

From out of nowhere, two police horses appeared and I heard one of the offices screaming into his radio, 'We have a code red, a code red.' It was a call for reinforcements. I was as scared as I have ever been in my life.

The mounted police officers managed to get us to another street and pushed us against a wall, where they told us to stay. My fellow Rangers supporters were still singing their songs but, by now, the police were threatening to arrest them. The police kept us there for 40 minutes while the Celtic fans dispersed, then one of the officers warned, 'Right, you are on your fucking own now.'

So here I am in the middle of Parkhead, still surrounded

by all these clowns, and a long way from safety. Nobody had recognised me but I now knew that I had to get away from them. I went to the front of the group because I figured that, if anything untoward happened, I could run away from the trouble.

Thankfully, by now there were only small pockets of Celtic fans, although my group wanted to fight every one we came across. Eventually there was just one last Celtic pub to walk past, after which I could feel safe again. Inevitably, as we approached this pub, the guys I was with resumed their singing and started throwing stones at the pub. That was my signal to run as fast as I could go. I glanced back only to see dozens of Celtic supporters tumble out of the pub, to give the group of Rangers supporters the hiding they had been threatening to give them.

I only felt safe when I arrived at Duke Street, home of the Louden Tavern. Many of you may associate the word 'tavern' in your mind with the image of a thatched-roof inn with ancient wooden beams and a roaring log fire. The reality of the Louden Tavern is a blue building emblazoned with slogans like 'The Greatest Pub In The World', 'The Most Famous Pub In Scotland' and, most tellingly, 'We Are The People'. In short, it is the Glasgow Rangers supporters' pub, and not a place to be seen if you are wearing anything green.

The result of my nightmarish experience that Sunday afternoon in August 2000 was that I got back to Mum's about an hour and a half late. She had got herself into a right state worrying that something dreadful had happened to me. I never have been back to Celtic Park and I never will.

CHAPTER NINE

GOING UP IN THE WORLD

Apart from my Celtic Park nightmare, I had a decent year in 2000, when I played in the final stages of several tournaments and continued to accumulate ranking points. But a real breakthrough in my professional career came in time for the 2001–02 season, with the news that I had cracked the top 16. I had my place among the elite, alongside the likes of Ronnie O'Sullivan, Stephen Hendry and John Higgins. I had finally reached the Holy Grail and a huge weight had been lifted from my shoulders. It had taken a long time – too long, really – but when I got there I vowed that I was going to stay there.

There was a downside to this sort of exposure – I was attracting some negative press. Although the press never quite said it directly, I felt they were portraying me as an intruder and as someone who would be lucky to stay in the top 16 for a second season. It was an insinuation that annoyed Alex, in particular. Now, it meant that, as well as maintaining the standard of my snooker, I had to adopt something of a siege mentality. It was Alex and I against the world.

Despite such negative press coverage, which had made me nervous, the new season had started well. In October 2001 I was thrilled to reach the final of the first ranking tournament of the season – the British Open at Newcastle. I may have lost to John Higgins in that final but, at least, the points I picked up more or less assured me of my place in the elite group for the following season. It's like a European Tour or PGA Tour golfer – if they can get a win or a second-place finish under their belt early in the season, it takes all the pressure off because it means they have already secured their playing rights for the following year.

Funnily enough, although it was only my second final, I do not have too many memories of the actual tournament. I beat Joe Perry and Ali Carter along the way, and I gave John a good match in the final. He beat me 9-6 but the frame he took to win the match could have gone either way. If I had managed to pinch it and get the score back to 8-7, who knows what might have happened?

It was certainly a huge improvement on my previous appearance in a final, in the Regal Scottish Masters at Aberdeen in 1999, when Stephen Hendry had drubbed me 9-1. He had been a huge favourite to win then and it was the same again when I took on John but, this time, I proved to myself and to some of my fiercest critics that I could survive at this level.

Losing is never nice but it is quite difficult to be disappointed or to be too hard on yourself if you have lost to somebody who is so obviously better than you are. The cheque was for about £30,000 so that represented another boost for the bank balance and, once again, it made me all the more determined to find a way to win a tournament.

It was great to get the money but I have never been the sort of person to look at a cheque and think, Right, I am now going to go out and blow a huge proportion of this on the latest CD sound system, a massive HD-ready TV, home cinema and state-of-the-art computer system. I have always kept one eye on the future and it is important to me to know that I have some money in the bank.

At that time there were nine or ten tournaments, which meant there were only nine or ten opportunities to earn prize money. More recently that number has fallen to six so there is a limit to how much can be won. All I could do was to keep battling away. I was picking up ranking points here and there, and reaching the occasional quarter-final but, all the same, I was failing to set the world on fire.

CHAPTER TEN
CHINA CRISIS

*I*n 2002 I was due to fly to the Far East with Alex Junior to play two tournaments: the China Open in Shanghai and a second tournament in Thailand's capital city of Bangkok. I must admit that I don't like going to the Far East much – I hate the food and I normally struggle to sleep – but I do recognise that China, in particular, represents a huge growth area for the sport and that, for as long as we have tournaments in that part of the world, I will be happy to go and play in them.

The plan was that we would catch a flight from Glasgow to London, then fly from London to Shanghai but, when I looked out the window on the day of departure, there was snow everywhere. That is not unusual in Scotland but it hadn't been forecast and it took me by surprise.

Alex picked me up and dropped Alex Junior and I off at Glasgow airport but the heavy snow was still pelting down and the departure boards showed that no flights were taking off. I was confident that the airport workers would be able to get the runways cleared and that we would soon be on our way but the snow was so heavy that, as fast as it was being removed from the tarmac, it was being replaced by more. As time ticked by I began to grow anxious about whether or not we were going to be able to catch our connecting flight.

A one-hour delay became a two, then a three-hour delay. Finally the runways were clear of snow and we were told that we could board our flight but, by now, I knew we didn't have a prayer of reaching Heathrow in time for the Shanghai flight. And sure enough, on our arrival at Heathrow, taxiing towards the terminal building, I could see our intended Thai Airlines flight already disappearing into the sky.

The next flight to China was some 11 hours away. To make matters worse, they couldn't guarantee us a seat on the plane because it was full and our only hope was that somebody didn't turn up. It also meant that we had to be there so that we could sort everything out in the event that seats were made available for us. Normally we would fly business class, which means that you can wait for your flight in the VIP lounge, but we didn't even know if we were going to be able to board the plane, never mind worry about how comfortable our seats were going to be. And that meant they wouldn't let us into the VIP lounge either.

Alex Junior and I hated every minute of our 11-hour wait. We were relieved when we were offered two seats after a cancellation. Thank God for that. But the flight was going to Bangkok, which meant that, when we got there, we would need to catch another plane to take us on to Shanghai. And remember, I can't stand the place.

After a flight that seemed to take for ever, we touched down in Bangkok, collected our luggage, then faced a further five hours for the flight to Shanghai. The two of us were wrecked so we decided that we had to find somewhere to put our heads down and get some sleep. We found a hotel nearby, which was absolutely filthy and, under normal circumstances, I wouldn't have gone anywhere near it. The bedding was so bad that I refused to get in between the sheets, so I just lay on top of it and dozed off for a couple of hours.

Even after our five-hour flight from Bangkok to Shanghai, our journey still wasn't quite complete – there was still a one-hour bus ride to our hotel. In all it had taken 42 hours and you will not be surprised to learn that neither Alex Junior nor I were exactly at the peak of our powers. We were shattered and we had arrived a full 24 hours later than scheduled. That night we went to bed and tried to sleep but our body clocks were out of synch and we got up very early on the morning of the day when I was playing my first match, which was scheduled to start at 2.30pm.

We had breakfast but I didn't want to go back to my room because I was worried that, if I sat down, I would fall asleep. 'Right then, Alex. We are going for a walk,' I announced. And off we went through the streets of Shanghai, which was hardly a relaxing preparation for that afternoon's match.

On our return, at around 11am, Alex Junior was really struggling to keep his eyes open. The venue wasn't far from the hotel and we still had three hours to kill. What harm could it do to have a quick nap? I knew that I couldn't play snooker in this state. I had to get some rest. So we set the hotel room alarm clock, as well as the alarms on our phones. What could possibly go wrong?

The next thing I was aware of was the sound of a doorbell being rung, over and over and over again. It was a member of the hotel staff, frantically trying to rouse us. I looked across at Alex and he was still sound asleep, then I looked at the clock. I remember thinking, Quarter past two – that can't be right. I play at half two. And then, suddenly, I knew that we had slept in. Screaming at Alex to get up, I flew across the room and opened the door to find a receptionist, who had been ringing the room phone for ages in an effort to rouse us.

By now I was in a blind panic. I grabbed my trousers, my shirt and my waistcoat, and put them on. I had no pants or socks on but, at least, I had the presence of mind to pick up my snooker cue. I raced through the hotel lobby and out of the building but there was no courtesy car available. I managed to stop a taxi.

Picture the scene. I don't speak Chinese and the taxi driver didn't speak English, but he knew who I was and he knew where I wanted to go. I had been to the venue before and I realised very quickly that he was taking me the wrong way. He was also taking his time. I was screaming at him, telling him to hurry up, but I was wasting my breath. I eventually told him to pull over, threw some Chinese money at him and got out of the taxi. He must have thought I was stark-raving bonkers. I had a vague idea where I was and ran the rest of the way.

I was 15 minutes late and you can imagine the state that I was in. No socks, no pants, my hair all over the placed, unwashed, unshaven, covered in sweat, my shirt undone. Mike Ganley, the tournament director, was waiting for me and I told him that I had to go to the toilet for a quick wash.

'Graeme, you can't,' he said. 'You need to go straight in. You are already two frames down.'

I had been penalised two frames for being late. The choice facing me was a stark one. If I went to the toilet, I would be docked a further frame. I was playing Darren Morgan, who is an obdurate opponent at the best of times, and I knew that I couldn't give him a three-frame start, especially not in a best-of-nine encounter.

My head was spinning. It's like being late for a tee-off time in golf, where you rush to the first tee and hit a shocking opening drive, and it takes you several holes to get your act together. And that is precisely the way it was for me during this match.

I walked into the arena and was aware that some of my fellow professionals were enjoying a right good laugh at my expense – and who could blame them? They'd all heard about the 42-hour journey so I guess it didn't take them long to work out that I'd slept in.

I broke off in the third frame, only for Darren to promptly make a frame-winning break, so I found myself 3-0 down without playing a single shot. But at least I could go to the toilet and have a quick wash and, by this time, Alex Junior had arrived, complete with clean socks and pants for me. I put some water on my hair and somehow managed to make myself look presentable.

My game improved. Somehow I won the next three frames and was level pegging with Darren. I even found myself thinking, What a story this will be if I manage to win. But it wasn't to be. He beat me 5-3.

My hatred for China and Thailand was complete. Part of

the problem back in those days was that I didn't really mix with the other players, whereas now I get on well with the likes of John Higgins and Stephen Maguire so I don't mind being away from home. We sit and play cards now but back then I used to spend all my spare time in the hotel watching TV, and it wasn't a good experience.

The other thing is that, if you get knocked out in the first round, you have to spend the rest of the week cooling your heels, waiting for the tournament to finish so that everybody can climb aboard another plane and fly on to Thailand, where it all begins again. So I was like a bear with a sore head. I have no idea how Alex put up with me for the rest of that week.

It didn't take long for the story to get out and it was all over the newspapers. The readers of the *Herald* newspaper in Scotland voted it the funniest sports story of the year. I didn't see the funny side of it at the time – but I do now.

CHAPTER ELEVEN

RIGHT ON CUE

*T*here was a time in my career when I played while wearing a sticking plaster on my chin. Many people thought that I had worked out a routine whereby when a certain part of the cue reached the plaster it was the signal for me to start my release. I am happy to reveal here and now that that theory is absolute rubbish.

My parents had bought me a cue from Reardon's snooker club and I had used it for many years. That one had been a smooth ash cue but a replacement cue had some indentations and, if I didn't shave, the cue irritated my skin and sometimes caused it to bleed. So the purpose of the plaster was to prevent that from happening. I know it wasn't the coolest look but I had to do something.

Commentators and pundits got it into their heads that there was an ulterior motive but there wasn't. It definitely wasn't a fashion statement. The funny thing is that I don't ever remember anybody asking me, during TV or newspaper interviews, why I was wearing the plaster. Maybe it was more fun for them to come up with their own reasons, rather than knowing the plain, simple and extremely boring truth. Nowadays I would probably approach Elastoplast and ask if they were interested in sponsoring me!

You may be wondering what happened to my original cue. Once again, all sorts of stories circulated in the media and most of them were miles off the mark so this is a good opportunity to set that record straight once and for all.

I was going through probably the worst patch of my career by early 2004. That January, Alex and I were driving back to Larkhall after I had been beaten by Dominic Dale in the Welsh Open, where I couldn't pot a ball. I was hopeless and, to be frank, I was in despair about ever finding my form again. I was losing to players that I should have been having for breakfast, and I felt that my love and passion for snooker were ebbing away at an alarming rate.

We stopped at a motorway service station and I said to Alex, 'I can't hit a barn door. Maybe it's time that I tried a new cue. What do you think?'

'Aye, that might be an idea but, if you are going to do that, you should break the one you are using now, just so that you can't go back to it.'

When the press got hold of the story they made out that I had smashed my cue in a fit of rage. Nothing could have been further from the truth. If I had kept it and struggled with a new cue, I would simply have gone back to it. Snooker cues are not like tennis rackets – it is almost impossible to find two that are the same.

I realised that Alex's suggestion had some merit. While he

sat in the service station having something to eat, I went out to the car, took out the cue and tried to break it over my knee but I couldn't. That just made me all the more determined so I ended up putting my foot through it a couple of times and then there was no going back. Watching me destroy that cue was a man sitting in a nearby parked car and he nearly choked on the sandwich he was eating when he saw what I was doing. He must have thought that I was a complete lunatic.

I no longer had a cue and my game against John Higgins in The Masters at Wembley was only 11 days away. On reflection, what I'd done may have been somewhat short-sighted. I had a friend in Larkhall called Andy Gibbs, who makes cues, so I phoned him and asked if he had anything lying about that might be suitable.

He asked me up to his house and duly produced a number of cues for me to look at – maybe ten in total. They were all nice enough but none of them felt quite right and then I noticed one propped up behind his sofa. It wasn't one he wanted me to have because it was small and it was light. To be frank, it was horrible but, for some reason, the second I picked it up I just knew that it was the one for me.

'I like this one, Andy.'

'You can't like that cue, Graeme. These are proper cues; they are much better – that one is awful.'

'It feels right. Do you mind if I take it and go and hit a few balls with it?'

'Of course not but I can't believe you are seriously considering using it. When you decide that you can't get on with it, pop back in and you can try one or two of these other ones instead.'

I started practising with the cue at the club in Larkhall and I instantly rediscovered my touch and my form. Suddenly, snooker was no longer a slog for me and balls were flying in from all angles. I had this image in my mind of poor Andy, having offered me the choice of the best cues that he had, shaking his head in despair as I cleared up with this awful piece of timber.

I went to The Masters and, although John beat me by the odd frame in 11, I felt good about my game again, so I went home and worked as hard as I have ever done. I practised relentlessly and regained my appetite for snooker. I know now that I had become lazy and that cue was the key to turning my fortunes around.

Just before the start of the 2009–10 season, the cue eventually broke. I sent it to a company in London for repair but they called me to say it was beyond hope.

'Graeme, please don't take this the wrong way,' said the man, 'but we would never have used this wood on a snooker cue. It's just terrible. The wood was diseased and it should have been thrown away. It is, without doubt, the worst cue I have ever seen in the possession of a professional snooker player.'

It might well have been sub-standard but it transformed my fortunes and I used it to reach the final of the World Championships. And I still have the bits from my original cue to remind me of the bad old days.

CHAPTER TWELVE

SO NEAR...

After losing 10-9 to James Wattana back in 1997, I began to wonder if I would ever return to The Crucible in Sheffield for the World Championship. My next opportunity came in 2000 and, wouldn't you know it, I was drawn against Steve Davis. By then he was already considered a veteran, but here was a man who had won the World Championship six times. Although he was no longer quite the crowd favourite as he was in his glory days, the fans still loved him and were desperate to see him win. He duly won 10-6, a defeat that hurt, because I should have been able to beat him.

It was much the same story in 2001. I had another nightmare draw, against John Higgins this time. He was absolutely flying and he sent me home after a 10-4 defeat. Three appearances, three first round losses. Would I ever win a match at The Crucible?

In 2002 I finally got off the mark, beating Finland's Robin Hull 10-6, but then I came up against Higgins again and he annihilated me 13-2. It was embarrassing. A year on I reached the second round again after beating England's Robert Milkins 10-4, but this time Ken Doherty narrowly beat me 13-12.

And so we arrived at The Crucible in April 2004. I agreed to sport a Hilton Hotel logo in return for them agreeing to give Alex, Dad and I a room for the duration of the tournament. By now my father wasn't working so he used to come to most of the tournaments with Alex and me.

My first match in 2004 was against Mark King. He is like a limpet and he never, ever knows when he is beaten. My recent form had been dreadful and so had his. I won 10-9 but only because I wasn't quite as bad as he was. Having won, I was scheduled to play Ryan Day or John Higgins next and their match also went to the deciding frame. Higgins should have lost but, like me, he scraped through by taking the final game. As John had thrashed me there two years earlier, I feared history would repeat itself after the way I'd played against King, so I had to account myself well.

I won the first session 5-3. Back at the hotel I switched on the television just in time to hear the pundits discussing my match and saying they were sure I would be kicking myself that I wasn't further ahead because John hadn't played well. What planet were these guys on? I was two frames ahead of John after the opening session and I was delighted. I certainly wasn't kicking myself, although I felt like kicking the television.

I won the second session 5-3 as well, which meant that I was now 10-6 in front and I was quietly confident that it would be enough, as long as I didn't do anything stupid. But now I felt under pressure. I only needed to win three more frames but I'd had a bad season and knew before the World Championship had even begun that I had to reach the quarter-finals, at least to preserve my status in the top 16. In other words, losing to John Higgins was not an option.

When we returned for the third and final session I don't mind admitting to you that I was pretty nervous. Higgins is a great player, easily capable of reeling off four or five frames in quick succession, and I couldn't let him do that. The key was to make a good start and, when I won the first two frames to go 12-6 in front, I thought that I was home and dry so I started to relax. Then Higgins found his form and began potting balls for fun to reduce the gap to 12-8 at the interval.

I only required one more frame for victory but, when we came back, John won the next frame, then the next. The gap was closing fast: 12-10. Fearing the worst, I was starting to twitch really badly but I managed to make a 62 break in the next frame, leaving John requiring a snooker. He is a class act and, when he came back to the table, he tapped it to acknowledge both the break I'd made and the position I'd left him in. On this occasion there was no way back for John.

I had finally reached the third round at The Crucible. To beat John Higgins in any tournament was an achievement but to do it here in Sheffield was massive for me. For years I had told everybody how much I loved the place and now it was time to show how far I could go in the World Championship.

I don't know about other players but, when I get to a tournament and go through the draw, I always look one round ahead to see who I might face in the next round and I knew that, if I could get past Higgins, next up would be either David

Gray or Lee Walker for a place in the last four. I would be lying to you if I didn't say that I fancied my chances against either of those players, even though David is a quality player.

In the event, I played Gray in the quarter-final and, for once in my life, I had a pretty comfortable passage through the match, winning the first session 6-2, then 11-5, before going on to beat him 13-7.

All was well in my world. I had reached the semi-finals of the sport's premiere event and I had retained my top-16 berth. Or so I thought. I was talking to a couple of journalists and they warned me that Ian McCulloch, who was in the other half of the draw, could still pip me. Fortunately, Stephen Hendry did me a massive favour by beating McCulloch 13-3 but a new set of calculations had been done and I now had to reach the final to remain a top-16 player. Oh no!

The most difficult opponent I could possibly have faced at the time was Matthew Stevens, the Welshman who had gone on to achieve all these wonderful things, leaving me trailing in his wake. And guess who I met in the semi-final?

Apart from anything else, Matthew is a good friend and here we were playing for a place in the final. I was about to get my first taste of what it was like to play in The Crucible with just one table in the arena, knowing that all eyes would be bearing down on me. I remember somebody telling me a story about Stephen Hendry playing in the semi-finals in Sheffield in 1997, when somebody in the audience tried to open a packet of sweets while holding a can of drink. The bag burst open, spilling its contents all over the floor, while the can flew into the air and landed with a thump. Everybody in the auditorium responded to the commotion – everybody, that is, bar Hendry, who was so focused on the shot he was playing that he heard nothing. And that is the sort of level of concentration that is required if you are going to have any chance of winning.

I watched the workmen take the second table out and rearrange things so that there was just the one match table left and now the arena looked much, much larger.

Suddenly there were lots of demands from television and the press, who all wanted to know how I felt about taking part in my first Sheffield semi-final. How did I think I would cope with the nerves? Did I think I could win? If I did win, could I go on and pick up the title?

There are some players who hate doing television interviews and, given the choice, I would not necessarily want to do them but they are part and parcel of what I do for a living so I always try to give sensible, well thought-out answers. I know that the last thing they want to hear when they ask a question is 'Yes' or 'No'. So I think about what I am going to say and always try to provide value for money. Sometimes you have to bite your tongue at the stupidity of the questions that come your way. For instance, 'Graeme, have you always wanted to play in the one-table situation here at The Crucible?' For a split second, but only for a split second, I was tempted to say, 'No, never,' to that one – but I resisted.

Reaching the semi-final was a big deal and it brought it home to me that here I was with the opportunity to achieve a lifetime's ambition, with a chance to make Alex, my parents, my brothers, my aunts and uncles, and Elaine proud of me. Perhaps even Mrs McDonald, my art teacher back at school, might have afforded herself a little smile and been able to admit that maybe she was wrong after all. All sorts of thoughts run through your mind in a situation like this but it is essential to remain in the present, not to let your thoughts drift.

At the time, I played for the Berries pub pool team back in Larkhall. The team all travelled down to Sheffield to watch the semi-final and cheered every good shot that I played. I struggle to describe the atmosphere over the two days the semi-final was played but all the clichés seem to fit well enough. If ever an atmosphere can truly be 'electric', it was for our match.

Matthew and I had both come a long way since our days in the juniors together. He was a red-hot favourite to win and he had lots of Welsh fans in the crowd, but they were fair to both of us and I thought that showed some class. People clapped and cheered at all the right times but never when either of us was over a shot. But if I missed a shot, before the balls had even come to rest you would hear his allies in the crowd shouting, 'Come on, Matthew! Go on, son!' It brought out the best in us both.

I won the first session 5-3. If I am honest, I have to say that the snooker in those opening frames was not great but, from that point on, we both caught fire. And how.

Matthew played outstanding snooker. He hit me with break after break after break. If I missed a ball, I knew that the frame was as good as over. But he couldn't win the session. Somehow, I managed to get out of the second session at 4-4, so I was leading 9-7 and I know that he must have been thinking, What do I have to do to get in front of this guy? I felt that he had battered me, so I knew how he must have been disappointed.

The third session was an action replay of the second. Once more he seemed to make a break whenever he got to the table. I won the first frame of that session to extend my lead to three frames, but Matthew then came storming back with three fabulous big breaks and suddenly we were level: 10-10.

In my head I could hear the commentators and the journalists starting to write me off. I knew they would all be expecting him to kick on and win but it simply made me all the more determined to stay with him. He took the next to lead but I won the last 3 frames of the session to lead the semi 13-11. It didn't matter what he did, I just kept coming back at him.

I required four frames to secure my place in the final, while he needed six. The tension was unbearable. I thought I'd finally got him when I extended my lead to 15-12, but back he came again to level it up at 15-15. By this time the crowd were beside themselves. What a match.

I won a scrappy frame to go one in front but he was in the middle of a decent break in the next frame and I had written it off and was getting ready for what I was convinced was going to be the 33rd and final frame, when he missed a ball. I came to the table and made a good break of my own to get back in the frame. After a safety exchange, he left me the blue and the pink to win the frame and the match. The blue and pink were easy shots but I spent ages over both of them, thinking, Right then, Graeme, this is to get into the final of the World Championship so, whatever you do, don't miss.

What a feeling when that pink disappeared into the pocket. I couldn't believe it was happening to me. It was a heck of a journey for that little boy who had watched the final all those years before on a black-and-white television in his bedroom while trying to imagine that he was Steve Davis. I had seen many others compete in those marathon 35-frame finals at The Crucible and now I was going to be doing it for real.

The place was in uproar and everybody was slapping me on the back and congratulating me. There were lots of live interviews to do between my semi-final win and the final. On the day of the final, I even agreed to take part with Elaine – pregnant with our son Lewis at the time – in a profile piece for TV, for which we were taken up to the hills overlooking the city of Sheffield. I can't believe that I agreed to do it – and I wouldn't do it now – but in 2004 all of this was new to me and I thought it was the done thing. Nevertheless, I had to keep reminding myself that I had a final to play.

The other semi-final was a huge anti-climax, with Ronnie O'Sullivan destroying a sadly out-of-touch Stephen Hendry 17-4 with a full session to spare. It meant that Ronnie had reached the final without breaking sweat.

More recently, Ronnie said that he hadn't played well for something like 17 years but I am here to tell you that, when I faced him in that final, he produced some of the finest snooker I have ever seen. It didn't help that I was still feeling the after effects of my semi-final with Matthew but I can put my hand on my heart and say that it wouldn't have made a blind bit of difference if I had been given a week to prepare for that match; I couldn't have beaten him and I don't believe that anybody else could. He had beaten Stephen Maguire 10-6 in the first round, Andy Hicks 13-11 in the second round and Anthony Hamilton 13-3 in the quarter-finals, before engaging with his demolition job of Hendry.

I have never seen anybody play as well as Ronnie did that

year. Some of his opponents get annoyed when he switches to play left-handed during frames, whereas I believe it simply shows what a genius he is. He is so good left-handed that I often don't even notice that he has switched. In saying that, I would rather he played me left-handed right from the off because I believe I may then have a better chance of beating him. I couldn't hit the cue ball left-handed, never mind pot a ball.

I have faced him when he has thrown his toys out of the pram and that is better for me because I know I can beat him if his mind is not on the job. But there was no messing about in that final. I told the press beforehand that I didn't think I had a chance of beating him but I admit that I was playing some mind games, hoping that he might hear what I'd said and maybe not try too hard. Deep down, before we began the final, I knew that I had a good chance of winning. There were only two of us and he wasn't the only one who had played well. You don't reach the final at Sheffield by accident. Sure, you may play the odd scrappy frame but you need to demonstrate sustained excellence – and I had done that.

Ronnie, on the other hand, had demonstrated sustained genius and continued to do so in the final. I might be able to handle him now, but not then. I learned more from that match than from any other game I have played. Without that experience, I would not have become the player I now am.

People regard Ronnie as an awesome potter and he is but, when his head is in the right place and he is concentrating and is fully switched on to what he is doing, he has a safety game to die for. His touch and feel are unbelievable. Time and again I came to the table and had no shot.

It was like a chess player taking on a chess computer that plays the game two or three levels above the standard he is capable of playing at – no matter what he tries, he will never beat the computer. I would look around the table and there wasn't even a safety shot available to me. I felt like a little boy lost who didn't know what to do – and I have never felt that way before or since on a snooker table. Yes, there are days when your touch isn't there but this was different. He was able to out-think me in every single aspect of the game. There was no luck involved either. Whenever I made a mistake, or gave him the slightest glimpse of a long red... *Bang!* Frame over. Another step nearer the exit. In those sorts of situations, you think, OK, that's one frame gone but that's fine because there's still a long way to go... Right, that's another frame gone but there's still no cause for panic... Oh dear, he's won another frame and that's the session over. This isn't looking so good after all.

I started strongly, winning the first five frames, but I only won another three after that and he ended up beating me 18-8. That result may look like a slaughter but I did give him a game. At the end of the first day he was 9-7 in front and, at that point, it looked like either one of us could finish up on top. I took a great deal of satisfaction from that performance but I knew that I couldn't sustain it. I was certain that he could.

I always had this feeling in the pit of my stomach that, if I had been able to get on even terms with him, he would have been able to move up a gear. When he went 12-8 ahead I knew that I had nothing left in the tank. I have had that feeling since then but it was a new experience for me at that time.

It meant that, for the final six frames or so, I was just going through the motions, trying to limit the damage but knowing that I was wasting my time. At the end of frames I would take a toilet break and try to give myself a good talking to but there was nothing there. I couldn't even summon up any feelings of anger. If the match had been close, adrenalin would have kept me going but I just wanted the end to come so that I could get out of there.

There are times when you go to the well and there is nothing there. It is not a nice feeling, especially when you are playing somebody like Ronnie O'Sullivan in the form he was in. I do not remember him going for a single shot that he should have left alone, and it takes incredible levels of discipline and concentration to do that for two days.

I sensed that the crowd were desperate for me to win a couple of frames and I wanted to oblige. Instead, I thought, 'If he lets me in, I am going to miss. Please, just let it be over. Clear up, get the frame won and let me get out of this place.'

It was the last way in the world that I had wanted to feel when we started the match. I couldn't focus, I was drained and I was exhausted. It would be easy to blame it all on the effort I had put into my semi-final but it was more than that. Yes, there was the fact that my opponent was in a different league but I believe that sometimes you have to go through experiences like this so that you can learn from them and come back stronger the next time you are put in the same position.

As a loser in a final, nobody really wants to talk to you – it is almost as if they feel that they have to go through the motions. I accept that it is part and parcel of being in a world final though, so I said my bit for the BBC and then had to go and face the rest of the media, when all I wanted to do was get out of The Crucible.

Oh, yes – and then there was the drugs test, which is something that happens to both competitors after every final. It is all well and good but there are occasions when you can't give them a urine sample and you have to wait with the tester until such time as you can. There are also random tests throughout the season. I was tested quite a lot one season and started to think that they were singling me out but they weren't.

There is a dinner after the final and it was the last place on earth I wanted to be but I did go, albeit fairly briefly. I just wanted to spend some time with Elaine and my family and friends. And I wanted to get my head down and get some sleep because I was shattered. I woke up the following morning and felt as if I had been hit over the head with a sledgehammer. My dream was over – the World Championship had been and gone. The table would be dismantled and all trace of that year's tournament would be gone from both The Crucible and the city of Sheffield. It also meant that the season was over.

I took many positives away from Sheffield but, in the aftermath of the final, I was not happy that I had been beaten, even though people who knew about snooker would know that I had given Ronnie a game for a day. I had proved to myself and to the world that I could cope at that level, although I knew that, if I ever reached the final again, I would have to find a better way of getting through a match like that. I had managed to do that in the semi-final; I had beaten one of the best players in the world in Matthew Stevens and I had retained my place in the top 16 when the chips were down.

When I got home to Larkhall I could not believe the reaction from the public. A party was staged for me, Scottish Television came along to speak to my friends and everywhere I went there was lots of back slapping. It was all very nice but I couldn't get away from one key fact – I had lost. I couldn't quite understand why people would want to celebrate the fact that I'd come second. I was touched by the show of support, of course, and I wondered what sort of reaction I would get if I was ever able to come home with the trophy. That, surely, would be the best feeling of all.

I made up my mind that I was going to find out. I decided that the next time the people of Larkhall put up some banners with my name on them, and the next time they were going to throw a party for me, it would be because I deserved it. And the only way that I could justify that sort of celebration would be to return home as world champion.

Meanwhile, domestic life was about to improve. During 2004 I had been reading a great deal about rocketing property prices so we got an estate agent in to value our house and I almost fell off my chair when he told us that he could market it at offers over £115,000. I looked at Elaine and she looked at me, and we both tried to play cool, saying, 'Yeah, that's kind of what we thought it might be worth.' We hadn't a clue. When we closed the door on him we both leaped up and down: 'We're rich, we're rich!'

We put the profit we made on the house and, later, a sizeable chunk of the money I got for finishing runner-up in the 2004 World Championship towards the house we are in now. It is funny how things go. We had an interest-only mortgage on our new home and it was a time when interest rates were being increased on a regular basis. We were struggling with the payments and then along came the 2004 World Championship, my appearance in the final and a runner's-up cheque for £125,000.

Alex also told me that he no longer wanted to take any part of my winnings. I was speechless but he explained that I had now got to the point in my career that he had always believed I would reach. He would still come to tournaments with me but now he would pay his way and I would pay mine. He was happy just to be with me, to be part of my success and to see me and his daughter living happily together.

The real highlight of 2004 arrived on 22 October, when Lewis, my son, was born. My snooker career was heading in the right direction, we had a fabulous family home and now we had a wonderful baby who has grown into a fantastic son. Being there for his birth was the best moment of my life.

What could possibly go wrong?

CHAPTER THIRTEEN

GETTING A BAD PRESS

I have never had an especially easy relationship with the media. Throughout my career, I always seem to have had more than my fair share of bad press. Knowing this, I shouldn't read the newspapers but I am afraid I can't stop myself, especially when you get somebody phoning you and saying, 'You should see what they have said about you in the *Daily Blah* today.' That is a like a red rag to a bull and I will go straight out and buy a copy of the offending paper.

It is difficult to know why they have given me a rough ride but I guess it has something to do with the way I play or, to be more accurate, the way that they perceive I play my snooker. I admit that I have been involved in my fair share of long frames and matches that have lasted too long, but answer me this question: if you were playing a crucial frame of snooker and your opponent kept putting the balls safe, would you take on an impossible shot that you might pull off once in a hundred attempts? And if you missed it and it was going to cost you the match, maybe even your place in the top 16, would you still go for it? I thought not.

The long matches I have been involved in have not been because I am a slow player. Sometimes a frame will drag on because I refuse to give up and I always want to make it as difficult as possible for any opponent to beat me. I take pride in making it very hard for anybody to win a frame against me – I would never give away a frame and that means that there is always the risk of drawn-out safety battles developing.

When I lose matches it is almost never 5-0; it is far more likely to be 5-4. If ever I do find myself three or four frames behind, they will have to scrape me off the table to beat me because I dig in and refuse to go away. I have actually been quoted many times as saying that I wouldn't like to play me. Another player who performs in such a way is Mark Selby. You think that you have got him beaten, either in a frame or a match, and he always seems to find a way to come back at you. But he doesn't get stick from the press.

Once you have been involved in a couple of marathon sessions you find yourself being tagged as a grinder. I find it quite offensive. Now Cliff Thorburn, he was a grinder. Not me though. I have never been one and I hate being described as such.

When you go to a tournament there is always a cuttings board. Anything that has been written about the tournament or the players will be cut out and pinned up on the board. It is a good way of working out how much coverage the sport is generating in the national press. I would read the *Racing Post* and, no matter who I was playing, the paper would advise its readers to back him to beat me. There was no justification for it.

I would read stuff like, 'Yes, Dott is in the top 16 but he is generally regarded as being the weakest player among the game's elite.' Regarded by whom – some journalist who had probably never even picked up a snooker cue? I would read these articles with a growing sense of anger and disbelief, and think to myself, Cheeky bastard!

On one occasion I was playing Marco Fu and he was odds-on with the bookies to beat me. I had no problem with that – when on form at that time, he probably deserved to be a slight favourite to edge me. All the same, it was a tough match to call and one journalist was urging readers to put their money on Fu winning. I was outraged. Not because I felt that I was a much better player than Marco, just that when you studied the odds and the form, there was very little between us. And when you have two evenly-matched competitors in any sport, you would rarely bet on the one who was odds-on. I remember thinking, How bad does this journalist think I am?

Then there was a time that Willie Thorne was talking about the number of strong Scottish snooker players. He reeled off about eight names but mine was not among them. 'Yes, the Scots have many, many great players. You've got Stephen Hendry and John Higgins, Stephen Maguire, Alan McManus, Billy Snaddon, Chris Small, Jamie Burnett and Ewan Henderson...' I wouldn't have minded but I was higher ranked than most of them.

There are times, too, when the snooker players-turned-commentators say things that are absolutely outrageous. They forget that they missed shots too. They forget that they were involved in sleep-inducing frames, especially the guys who were playing in the 1970s, when the standards were nowhere near as high as they are now.

Poor Alex would often end up raging at some of the things that were said during tournaments. Pundits would always try to find an excuse for the other player, rather than just accepting that, on the day, I had played better. If someone else like Ronnie O'Sullivan loses, there has to be a reason. Perhaps his head is not in the right place. Or maybe he is suffering from depression again. Could it be because he is tired? Or maybe, just maybe, he lost to the better man! Don't get me wrong here, O'Sullivan is a fabulously gifted player and, when he is in full flow, he is beautiful to watch but there are days when he is going to come up against an opponent who is playing better than him, and I just wish the commentators could accept that and give credit where it is due.

Alex wouldn't let it lie. If he heard something that he didn't like or that he didn't agree with, he would wait until the next time he saw the commentator who had made the remark and he would have it out with him.

And I have taken issue with Willie Thorne on a couple of occasions. If you listen to him, you will quickly realise that he is obsessed with big breaks. He always used to go on and on about all the maximum breaks he made on the practice table when he was in his prime. It got to the point where it put me off because I knew that, if he was commentating on my match and we went a couple of frames without either of us making a decent contribution, I could hear him in my mind talking about the need for a big break. I would get in among the balls and my thought process would be something like this: Right,

I've got a really good opportunity here but, if I don't make at least 80, Willie is going to slaughter me.'

It is hardly the ideal way to be thinking when you are trying to win a match, I am sure you will agree. I would rattle off 40, then I would put the green safe. In anybody's language, that is good, solid match snooker. I wasn't deliberately breaking down on 40 but, if I had run out of position, I just figured that it made sense to make life as difficult for my opponent as possible. And then, as I would walk back to my seat, in my mind I would hear Willie saying, 'Graeme Dott's missed a frame-winning opportunity there. He should have done better from that chance. He is not scoring enough. This is why he won't make it to the very top of the game.'

If Ronnie O'Sullivan does the same thing, on the other hand, he is a 'genius'.

I like Willie. In company, he is great fun and has always got lots of stories to tell. But the criticism about big breaks got to me and I have found it hard not to have a little dig, especially as it was coming from a man who never reached the semifinals of the World Championship, which means that he never played on a one-table situation at The Crucible. It is easy to play from the commentary box.

Neal Foulds is head and shoulders above the other commentators but, for reasons that I fail to understand, he doesn't get to commentate on as many games as he should. Apart from anything else, he is younger than the likes of Thorne, John Virgo and Dennis Taylor, so he is more in touch with what is going on in the game today. He was a top player into the 1990s and he knows what pressure is all about in the current game.

It seems unfair that the press and the commentators have never quite rated me as highly as I believe I should have been. I am not a prima donna and I don't have a massive ego; all I am asking for is the credit that my achievements deserve. I listen to them talking about players who have achieved half of what I have done and it is like they are talking about world champions – and that really annoys me.

Early in my career I had reached one final, a couple of semis and a quarter-final, and I felt I was making steady progress but then I would read an article that would talk about me failing to live up to my potential. It got to the point where Alex said to me, 'Listen, Graeme, I think we should stop buying the newspapers if we think they are going to be running a story about you.'

I knew where Alex was coming from and, once again, he had my best interests at heart but, in a way, all the criticism spurred me on and made me all the more determined to show the world what I could do. It fired me up.

Where I do the draw the line, though, is in reading internet forums where you get the general public expressing their views about you. Some of the stuff that is written on the internet is extremely hurtful, all the more so because it comes from people who don't know you and who have no idea what it is that makes you tick. They know nothing about your personal circumstances but still they feel able to write the vilest things about you. I know it goes on so I steer clear of it because, if I did read it, I know how much it would upset me.

Lastly, I get asked from time to time which referees I most respect. I really don't want to upset anybody here but the fact is that being a snooker referee is not that difficult. You just need to know the rules. If a player finds himself in a position when he is playing a series of misses as he tries to get out of a snooker, you need to be big enough to ask for help from the television referee if you are unsure where to replace the cue ball.

I don't have a problem with any snooker referees. The best ones are those who keep a low profile and who can apply a bit of common sense when things get tense. I have come across one or two who have got things wrong and have refused to admit their mistakes but I guess that is just human nature.

CHAPTER FOURTEEN
PRIZE HUNTER

*T*here are no certainties in life but I am as sure as it is possible to be that Paul Hunter would one day have become a world champion.

Paul had the lot. He was a great potter, a fabulous break builder and he possessed a great safety game. Oh yes, and he was also blond and incredibly good looking. Women loved him and so did his fellow players.

He beat Alan McManus in the UK Championship not long after turning pro and, in his first season, he became the youngest player to reach the semi-final of a ranking tournament when he got to the last four at the Welsh Open, aged 17 years and 3 months. What an achievement.

He was fined and docked ranking points in 1998 after testing positive for cannabis but those who may have thought that he was in danger of going off the rails were wide of the mark. I guess he was just a young boy who wanted to try these things. It has never appealed to me but I can understand why some people feel the need to have a go. Being caught out in that way was a wake-up call for Paul and he quickly knuckled down again, winning the 1998 Welsh Open at the age of just 19. Facing then-world champion John Higgins in the final, he won 9-5, achieving 3 century breaks in the match. It was tremendous snooker.

By the start of the 1999–2000 season Paul was already ranked 12 in the world and was destined for greatness. The guy had an aura, something he perpetuated with that wonderful story about the final of The Masters in 2001. He was trailing by 6-2 after the first session against Fergal O'Brien and told the assembled media that, during the interval, he and his then girlfriend, Lindsey, resorted to Plan B. In other words, they'd had sex. Rejuvenated, he returned to the Wembley Arena, reeled off four centuries in six frames and won the match. I have no idea whether or not it was a true story. I hope and suspect that it probably did happen because that is the kind of fellow Paul was. He loved the attention that he received afterwards, although he was ribbed mercilessly by his fellow players.

He returned to Wembley in 2002 and won the Masters title again. It was like he owned the place. Wembley crowds can be quite hostile to outsiders but, although Paul was from Leeds, they loved him to bits. He also won the Welsh Open in 2002 and it seemed that the sky was the limit.

And it just kept coming. He reached the semi-finals of the World Championships in 2003, a season during which he won a tournament and reached four semi-finals and three quarter-finals. It was the sort of level of consistency that most other players could only dream about. The following year he won his fourth Masters title, beating Ronnie O'Sullivan in a classic final, during which Paul scored 5 centuries to win 10-9.

By now Paul was No 4 and had the world at his feet. And then, in April 2005, he discovered he had cancer. He spent several months fighting the illness but I don't think many of his fellow professionals realised just how ill he really was. By October, when he competed in the Grand Prix, the weight had fallen off him and the chemotherapy had caused all his hair to fall out. It broke my heart to see him the way he was. He was clearly in a great deal of pain and you could only feel sorry for Rory McLeod, his opponent in the first round. I mean no disrespect to Rory when I say that, under normal circumstances, Paul would probably have blown him away... but these were not normal circumstances.

Two months after the Grand Prix, Paul won his only match of that season, beating Jamie Burnett in the UK Championship. I thank God that I was not drawn to play against him during that period because, knowing what he was going through, I don't know if I would have been able to hold it all together.

There was a sense of disbelief among the players when we had heard that Paul was ill in the first place. Cancer happened to people you didn't know and it definitely didn't happen to young men. Many of us believed he would come through it. I know that I thought, It will probably be like testicular cancer and they will be able to cut it out and he will be OK.

But he wasn't OK. He fought the illness all the way but eventually it got him. Paul died on 9 October 2006, only days before his 28th birthday. I was stunned. He was a great guy, with a fabulous wife (he married Lindsey in 2004) and a daughter born in December 2005. It was such a waste.

Tributes flooded in from all over the world and his name will never be forgotten as the Paul Hunter Foundation was set up after his death to give disadvantaged children places to play sport and socialise. A light went out the day he died.

CHAPTER FIFTEEN

ON TOP OF THE WORLD 2006

*F*eeling confident about my game, I began 2005 with the Malta Cup, held at Portomaso marina, near the island's capital of Valetta. After a 5-1 victory over England's Adrian Gunnell, I was up against Ronnie O'Sullivan in the second round and it didn't take long to work out that, although his body might have been there, his mind certainly wasn't. He was fidgeting in his chair and playing some ridiculous shots.

Hitting a 90-odd break in the first frame, I couldn't help thinking that I had a good chance of beating him: 'I don't think he wants to be here.' But why wouldn't anyone want to be in Malta? It is a beautiful island with a great climate and a population who love their snooker. There are few places where we snooker players are made to feel more welcome but it obviously wasn't an island where Ronnie wanted to be.

I made good breaks in the second and third frames so, before I knew where I was, I had opened up a three-frame lead. He got in at the start of the fourth and potted red, black, red, black, red... then he missed the black off the spot and conceded the frame. I was speechless but I wasn't going to complain at being 4-0 up in a best-of-nine encounter.

When we came back from the interval, I made another excellent break to win the match 5-0. Yes, he had stupidly conceded a frame to me but I had played very well and the frame he gave me had been his first opportunity to get in among the balls. All the same, the press write-ups gave me no credit for playing four frames of superb snooker – just about the one frame he handed to me, and that he had no interest in playing.

In the next round I faced the legend Steve Davis. I have nothing but admiration for the way the six-time former world champion has kept plugging away. Even though he was way past his prime in 2005, he remained a formidable opponent, although I beat him 5-1 in a scrappy quarter-final. It meant that I had reached the last four and had only lost two frames. I felt fresh as a daisy.

Then I ran into John Higgins. He won the first 3 frames, knocking in a 141 in the second and a 121 in the third. Here we go again, I thought to myself. I was certain that I was going to be on the next flight home, especially when he led 5-2, but I suppose that I threw caution to the wind after that. Against all the odds, I won 4 frames in succession to beat him 6-5 and now I was back in another final.

And my opponent? Stephen Hendry. It would be something of an understatement to describe it as a tense affair, but it most certainly was.

At the end of the second frame, I had scored the princely

total of 7 points; Stephen had won the opener 92-0 and the second 121-7, with the help of a 121 break. By the interval I had caught up and we were level-pegging, only for him to storm back by scoring 102. I pulled one more frame back, so that we were 3-3, before Stephen nudged ahead yet again, finishing the opening session 4-3.

When we resumed, I managed to take the opener with a break of 93 to level it up again but then it was as if Stephen was powered by jet fuel; he made his third century of the final and, when he took the next couple of frames as well, he led 7-4, needing 2 more for victory. I hadn't potted a single ball for three frames.

But I hadn't come all this way just to roll over. I put together breaks of 53, 83 and 59 to level things at 7-7 and, when Hendry took the next to go within one frame of victory, I refused to panic. He seemed to have the 16th frame won but I managed to lay two snookers on the yellow, one a fluke, the other quite intentional, in what turned out to be a marathon frame.

I was left with a tricky blue down the side cushion to win the frame and take the match into the final frame but I needed to use the rest and missed the pot. Hendry was out of his chair in an instant and pocketed blue, pink and black to win his 36th ranking event.

'When Graeme was mopping up the colours I was convinced it was going to be eight-all. I was so relieved when he missed the blue,' said Hendry afterwards. 'At seven-four I was cruising but at the end it could have swung either way. I'm delighted with this because over the week I've played very well.'

Afterwards I told the press, 'Battling is what I'm good at but it wasn't good enough today. I'm gutted. It's been a pleasing week but missing that blue was a horrible way to lose. If I'd potted it for eight-all, it was a toss of a coin.'

I don't know what it is with Hendry but I have never beaten him and, whenever we play each other, I always seem to bring out the very best in him. He can be playing rubbish against other players yet, when he plays me, suddenly he is a world-beater again. Losing that final in Malta hurt me badly. It is one thing to play badly in a final and lose but it is something quite different to play at your very best and find that you still can't win.

Would I ever bring home a trophy?

My first-round curse struck again at The Crucible in April 2005. At the World Championship I played Ian McCulloch, the man I had prevented from getting into the top 16 the previous year, and he beat me 10-9. The sense of anti-climax was huge. I thought that I had laid my Crucible bogey to rest and losing to McCulloch was never part of the plan.

McCulloch is a guy I have never enjoyed playing because I believe he is too slow. Fair play to him though – when the chips were down, he was good enough to win the decisive frame and send me packing. It was not a great way to end the season and it did not set me up for a great summer holiday but it did make me even more determined to ensure that it wouldn't happen when I got back there the following year.

Staying at the Hilton Hotel in Sheffield had worked for me in the 2004 World Championship so we booked in there again for the 2006 one, where I was seeded 14. By this time snooker was down to six tournaments and the prize money for The Crucible fortnight had fallen. When Ronnie O'Sullivan had beaten me two years earlier he collected £250,000 and I received £125,000 as runner-up. Now the winner's cheque had been reduced to £200,000, while the runner-up earned £100,000. I still thought it was a pretty fair reward but the warning signs were there for everybody to see.

I had Derek Hill with me in Sheffield. Everybody knows him as Big Del and he used to be Ronnie O'Sullivan's coach. He is a huge man who stands about 6ft 10in. For me, he was somebody to bounce ideas off, although he also kept an eye on my technique.

I arrived for the World Championship to learn the good news that I had drawn John Parrott in the first round. Parrott is a former world champion but he had dropped out the top 16 some years before and, although he was still putting himself through the qualifiers, he was by now spending most of his time working as a pundit and commentator. If I had played him three or four years earlier, I would have regarded it as a very difficult draw – but not now. I didn't expect him to provide me with a great deal of resistance and my hunch was to be correct. I played well and beat him 10-3.

I had been expecting to play Hendry in the second round but Derbyshire-born Nigel Bond caused a huge upset by beating the 7-time champion 10-9 in their opening encounter on a re-spotted black. Nigel is a very challenging opponent – it seems that, no matter what you do to him, he just keeps coming back. He is someone you want to meet early in a tournament because he sharpens you up. It was a tough match but I did what I had to do and came through it 13-9.

Next up, in the quarter-final, was Neil Robertson of Australia. I came out the traps well and, at 12-8, needed just one more frame to reach another semi-final. At the time Robertson's general approach of throwing caution to the wind and going for every possible shot had helped him beat Paul Hunter 10-5 in the first round and Stephen Lee 13-9 in the second. But that is the wrong sort of game for the World Championship and the time comes when that gung-ho approach can catch you out, when the balls don't drop into the pockets and the cue ball does not run safe. Of course, I was happy for him to play that way because I felt that I could always do enough to beat him over the best of 25 frames.

I tied him up in knots simply by playing a series of safety shots that left him with nowhere to go. Every now and again he would try an impossible pot, miss and I would clear up to win the frame. As far as I was concerned, he was playing right into my hands. If he was going to keep making the same mistakes, why should I change my approach?

In the event, it was Neil who decided to adopt different tactics. He was one frame from defeat and I guess he thought that he had nothing to lose. Where before he had played the occasional safety shot, now he had clearly made up his mind that, if he could see a ball, he was going to try and pot it.

Guess what? It began to work for him. In the blink of an eye 12-8 became 12-9. I still wasn't too concerned because there was no way he could keep doing it. Except that he did. He won the next and it was 12-10.

Our match was being refereed by Alan Chamberlain, who would never have been my first choice for match official. There was some history between us after a match against John

Higgins, when he called me for three fouls, claiming that my bowtie was touching the red. I was convinced it was impossible but what could I do other than accept the decision?

Robertson broke off and left me on the baulk cushion. I had a quick look and I could not see a red. Although there were plenty on the table, Neil had effectively snookered me. It meant that I had to be extremely careful with my escape because I didn't want to smash into the reds, bring them all out into play and leave him in among the balls again.

Before I go on, I need to explain that, if you can't see the object ball, you can have as many attempts to get out of a snooker as you want. However, if you can see a red and you miss it three times, it will cost you the frame. I should make it clear – I could not make direct contact with any red on the table.

I tried to play a two-cushion escape to clip the reds and bring the cue ball back to baulk but I failed to make contact, was called for a miss and Neil asked for the cue ball to be replaced in its original position because he wanted me to play again. Chamberlain placed the ball, by which time I had already made up my mind that I was going to try the same escape again.

The current score was a nerve-racking 12-10 and the only thing on my mind was where I was going to hit the cushion this time so that I could escape without causing too much damage. I played the same shot again off two cushions and missed it again. Chamberlain put the cue ball back and, as I was preparing to play the shot for the third time, Neil got out of his chair and said, 'He can see that red. He needs to be warned now.'

I hadn't a clue what he was talking about but I had a good look around the table and, sure enough, I had sight of a red. I turned to the referee and said, 'Well, you must have put the cue ball back in the wrong position, Alan, because I was snookered to start with.'

'No, no. I have put it back in the correct place.'

'You haven't,' I insisted. 'I was snookered on all balls. I would not have been playing this shot.'

He then pointed to the table and said, 'There's your chalk mark – that proves I am right.'

'I don't give a monkey's about where the chalk mark is – that mark is not from the first shot I played and is not where the ball was.'

At this point, Neil went back to his seat so I was left alone to argue my point. I was disappointed that he walked away. It takes an awful lot to get me angry and I had never argued with a referee in public before. I felt that I had been accused of cheating and it hurt. If I had been able to see the red ball in the first place, I would have played for it because it was a far easier shot than the one I was attempting. What infuriated me most of all was that I discovered later that all Alan Chamberlain had to do was speak to the television referee, who could have confirmed the exact spot where the cue ball had come to rest in the first place.

In the end I had no option but to go for the red and, of course, I caught it all wrong, let Neil in the balls and he cleared up. And now my lead had been reduced to 12-11 and I was raging. Sometimes you see two boxers and one catches the other with a punch, and you instantly know that the guy has gone. At that moment, I was gone. There was no way I was going to win that match. I sat in my seat feeling that the whole world was against me.

My head was spinning and all sorts of thoughts were going through my brain, such as, This referee doesn't like me, and, I can't believe that Neil has said what he has said.'

Next minute it was 12-all after another great break by Neil. This is just unbelievable, I thought to myself.

Somehow – and I really don't know how – I played well in the next frame. The adjoining table was clear so the partition had been raised and we had the eyes of the entire crowd on us. It all came down to the yellow. I had an extremely difficult safety shot, with the white in baulk and the yellow on a side cushion, and I tried to clip the edge of the yellow but missed it altogether.

Chamberlain quite correctly called a miss. Neil spent an age looking at what I had left him, which I couldn't understand because the obvious thing to do was to ask the referee to put the ball back and tell me to play again. It was a no-brainer, especially as I was sitting there thinking, I am going to play that shot again, hit the ball too thick and he is going to clear up and win. Thank goodness Neil couldn't read my mind. Instead of having the ball replaced, he got down to play the shot and I still expected him to stand up and tell Chamberlain, 'No, just put it back.' But he didn't. I was delighted.

He doubled-kissed it and left the yellow on. I couldn't wait to get to the table to pot the ball and win the frame and the match. But, boy, what an experience that was. Talk about grasping defeat from the jaws of victory. Robertson later said in a press interview that the reason he didn't put me back in was because he was convinced I would play a great safety shot and leave him in all sorts of trouble. If only he knew. Well, he does know now, I guess, so I am sure that he will not make the same mistake again.

The sense of relief after that quarter-final was immense and I went to speak to Mike Ganley, the tournament director, about what had happened earlier. Ganley confirmed that all the referees had the option of referring any dispute to the television referee. I said, 'Well then, Mike, I can't understand why you didn't let the players know, however, because I would have insisted that he check the television monitor.'

On such things destiny can be decided. Alan's decision was one that could have cost me the match and, as things turned out, had a huge impact on both my life and my career.

My sense of relief quickly disappeared when it was confirmed that I would be playing Ronnie O'Sullivan in the semi-final. He had thrashed Dave Harold 10-4 in the first round, before bettering Ryan Day 13-10 in the second round, then Welshman Mark Williams in the quarter-final. And now he stood between me and another final. It seems incredible that Ronnie wasn't the world No. 1 – but Shaun Murphy was. That's what the rankings said anyway.

I was looking forward to having another crack at Ronnie after our Crucible duel in the 2004 final. I just knew that I was a better player and I was ready for anything he could throw at me. That feeling all changed after the first session, which Ronnie won 5-3.

All the old self-doubts started to creep back in. Up until the semi-final I had been playing all right and there was nothing wrong with my tactics but it was my safety game that had got me through. Yes, I made some decent breaks and potted my share of balls but there was something missing. I felt that I was not quite firing on all cylinders. Against Ronnie I would play what I thought was a great safety shot and, not only would he find a way out, but he would hit me with an even better safety shot. I was starting to have visions of 2004 all over again. And I hadn't come this far to lose again.

Nothing was working but Big Del's coaching support was to prove invaluable. After that first session I said to Del, 'I don't think I can do this. I thought my safety play was good enough but I have just given him the best I've got and I'm losing five-three. Am I just kidding myself here?'

'You will come through, Graeme,' Del said. 'It is harder against Ronnie because he is so much better than the rest. Keep playing your safety game. If anything, you have to do it even more than you are. When you were playing Neil Robertson you only had to play two good safety shots before you got a chance. Against Ronnie you might need to play three or four safety shots. Treat it like an actual game and, believe me, if you win that part of the game – and you will – the match is yours for the taking. You will beat him.'

I wasn't sure if Del was saying this to me because he thought it was the right thing to say or because he genuinely believed it but it turned out that he was spot on. He knew what made Ronnie tick.

'I have coached Ronnie,' he said, 'and I know that he will not like it if you win the safety exchanges. He doesn't want to play that way; he wants to get in among the ball and make big breaks. If you win the safety game, you win the match.'

When we returned for the second session, I was ready for

a long, hard safety battle. And so it turned out. I played a safety shot, he came back with another. I played a safety shot, so did he. I hit another great safety shot, then he made a mistake! I felt like leaping out of my chair and saying, 'Yes! I've done it.'

As I went 7-6 in front, I missed something that the television cameras caught – Ronnie had the tip off the end of his cue. Now that is something you just don't do, especially in such a position, but he is a one-off and maybe he felt that he was losing momentum and could regain it if he forced an unscheduled break in play.

I saw Ronnie walking out the arena and wondered what on earth was going on. Jan Verhaas, the referee, wandered over and told me Ronnie had a problem with his tip, so I went back to the dressing room and waited with Del. And waited. And waited. I began to get angry at being messed about like this. Eventually I sought out the referee and asked, 'What are we waiting for? Are we expected to hang around until he finally finds a tip that he is happy with? How long is this going to take?'

'He is allowed fifteen minutes, Graeme.'

'He has had his fifteen minutes. I want to get back out there and start playing again.'

I was eventually told that play was about to recommence, so we went back into the arena and Ronnie didn't say a word to me. I would have expected some sort of apology or explanation but there was nothing at all. To be fair, it is possible that I play better when I have been needled, so he may actually have done me a few favours. I have never had a problem with the guy but I felt it would have been polite to have said something to me, especially as he had walked out of the arena in the first place without a word to me. It was rude.

Ronnie being Ronnie, though, he made a century in the very next frame, with a brand-new tip on his cue. That sort of thing doesn't happen to normal players. Sometimes his talent is just outrageous. It shouldn't be allowed!

As it turned out, I came out on top in the second session: 5-3. So we were all square at 8-8, not unlike we had been 2 years earlier, only this time I knew that I was the one who was on top. I was the one who felt better about the match position. Ronnie may not have agreed but I now believed that I was the favourite to win.

It felt like I was playing Rocky in the Sylvester Stallone film. He had come out and stamped his class on the contest, exactly as he had been expected to and then I had come back. Like all underdogs, I wasn't meant to give the champ a bloody nose but I had trained hard. In Del, I had a good man in my corner and I was listening well to what he was telling me.

Drawing Ronnie into a sustained safety battle was just like Rocky Balboa soaking up the best punches that the champion could throw at him before unleashing his own brutal attack. It may sound a trifle melodramatic but I felt I *was* Rocky and, the longer the semi-final went on, the more I was loving it.

I can do this, I thought. If I don't miss the chances when they come my way, I can beat this man. He is not invincible. I could also sense a growing wave of support for me from the crowd. They wanted to see somebody take this amazing player to the wire, to see how he would respond.

I am delighted to say that the contest didn't reach the final round and the judges' scorecards were not required. It was a brilliant feeling, as the second session closed, to know that I had gone from being 5-3 down to reassuring myself that I could win. It was a sure sign that my tactics were getting to him.

The third session was surreal. Nobody wins eight frames on the bounce against Ronnie, but I did. When he had beaten me in 2004, he didn't miss a single long pot – everything he went for he got. Overall, his game this time was just as good, with the exception of those long pots. I could tell that his inability to see off a long red was frustrating the life out of him. He was only missing by a fraction of an inch but that is the difference between losing and winning in both snooker and, indeed, most sports.

Behind the scenes, Del kept drumming home the message to me. 'Graeme, he can't pot a long ball,' he said. 'So if your safety is better than his, there is no way he can possibly win this match because he can't get in. When you get in, you are not missing and, even though you are not making huge breaks, you are doing enough – scoring forty or fifty, then putting the green safe, having another safety battle, winning that, then getting back in to make another break. It would be madness to change course.'

I knew he was right. But knowing it and going out and doing it were two very different things. I wanted to win, of course I did, but I wanted to make a few free-flowing century breaks of my own. There were times when I would look at a long red myself and I would be sorely tempted to have a flash at it – but I resisted.

For the first time in my life, I knew precisely what it meant to be 'in the zone'. I knew what I had to do and I went out there and did it. From eight-all I took three frames through employing these tactics and I began to sense that I had him right where I wanted him – the same way he had felt about me in that final two years earlier, I guess.

I am sure that many people in the crowd were surprised at what was happening. I am equally convinced, though, that some of them knew what I was doing and were impressed that I had worked out a game plan to beat this genius of the green baize. I had reached a stage where I was so focused on my own game that I was oblivious to anything Ronnie was doing.

I got it to 12-8 and then there was another short interval. Del had always said that my target for each mini-session like the one we had just played should be to finish two-all. Having rattled off those four frames, I was right on target and all I had to do was make sure that I took one of the next four and I would be certain to go into the deciding session with a lead. Right then, lad, I thought in the dressing room. The very worst that can happen is that we will finish twelve-all and you know that you would have settled for that before the match began.

All I had ever wanted was a chance to beat Ronnie O'Sullivan. This was fantastic. The match was being shown live on BBC TV in front of millions of people and there wasn't a spare seat to be found in The Crucible. Ronnie still had his fans but they were now quieter than normal because they sensed that their man might be in trouble.

I had a funny feeling and said to Del, 'If I can win this next frame to go thirteen-eight up, I reckon I will end up winning all eight frames in this session.' I knew Ronnie would come out and try to hit me right away so this 21st frame was crucial for me. If I could win it, I would knock the stuffing out of him. And that is precisely what happened.

So I felt pretty good walking out of The Crucible at the end of that session, as I was leading Ronnie by 16-8. All I had to do was win one more frame and I was in the final. But then, for no logical reason, I began to consider the possibility that, if I could win eight successive frames against him, there was no reason why he couldn't win nine on the bounce against me. Aaarrgh!

I hated the atmosphere that night. Yes, I was eight frames ahead but I didn't know what he was going to do. Would he throw caution to the wind? Would he try to beat me at my own game and set out to involve me in another safety battle? Naturally, almost everybody in the theatre was on his side. They hadn't paid their money to see one frame of snooker so, naturally, they wanted an O'Sullivan fight-back.

Before we came out and were waiting backstage, I noticed that Ronnie was holding a cue case. Normally he would have his cue in his hand so straight away I wondered what on earth he was up to. It entered my head that he might go to the table, open his case, it would be empty and he would concede. I wish I knew where these thoughts came from.

He had been pulling funny faces to the camera while I had been winning the eight frames in the previous session so it seemed to me that his head wasn't right and, when he is in that state of mind, he is capable of doing just about anything. But, of course, he did not concede. I later discovered that he had said he would give away his case and his cue after he had been knocked out of the tournament.

Naturally, everybody expected me to win and, when I missed a pot, all that I could hear around the theatre was a series of 'ooh's and 'aah's. It was all pretty light hearted but I still had to win that decisive frame to stumble over the line. The chances of losing were pretty remote but, if anybody was going to take the opportunity of beating me, it was Ronnie.

Inevitably, he won the first 3 frames and now it was 16-11, and there was a slightly different complexion to the match. If he had won the next to reduce the arrears to 16-12 at the interval, I would have been sweating. As it was, I won it on the black. I was in the World Championship final for 2006.

After the match, Ronnie duly put his cue into his case and handed it to a youngster in the crowd. In his post-match interviews he was fulsome in his praise for me, admitting that he had been outplayed. Yet, while I relished my win, I had not enjoyed that final session, mainly because I got the vibe from the spectators that they regarded the whole thing as a formality. They saw it as something of a joke and were shouting out things they wouldn't normally but I believed that I still had a job to do.

The press now took great delight in pointing out to me that I was now about to play in my fifth final and I still hadn't won one. I had lost to Stephen Hendry in Aberdeen, John Higgins in the British Open, Ronnie O'Sullivan in the 2004 World Championship and Hendry again in Malta. I felt there was nothing to be ashamed of: in those finals I had been beaten by the three best players in the modern era. Remember, too, that I was a huge underdog in every one of those matches.

It did get to me though. There would have something wrong with me if I hadn't sat myself down from time to time and asked whether I was ever going to win a tournament. There were demons messing with my mind. I thought about getting to a final and meeting somebody other than O'Sullivan, Higgins or Hendry – what would happen if I played a lower-ranked player and lost to them?

I didn't just want to win any run-of-the-mill event; I wanted to be world champion. I knew that I was going to be facing Peter Ebdon or Marco Fu. This is your time. Now it is your turn to become world champion, I told myself. You just have to go out and keep doing what you have been doing. Trust the game that has got you this far.

My opponent in the final did, indeed, turn out to be Ebdon, one of the toughest match players. I had played him five times previously and lost on every occasion. Ebdon's journey to the final had seen him beat Michael Holt 10-8 in the first round, David Gray 13-2 in the second and Shaun Murphy, the top seed, 13-7 in the quarter-final. But he wasn't really tested until his semi-final with Marco Fu, a match that went the distance before Ebdon triumphed 17-16.

When Peter first emerged on the scene he sported a ponytail and was a fluent potter. No nonsense. He won his fair share of matches but I guess that he felt he wasn't winning as many tournaments as he should have done, so he changed his style and became one of modern snooker's real grinders. He wasn't always pretty to watch but, boy, was he effective. Even when his game is below par, he is still very, very hard to get past. Despite all that, I fancied that I could beat him. Unfortunately, it turned out to be a dreadful final. I wish I could say otherwise – and neither of us chose to play poorly deliberately – but it was just one of those things.

When I had lost to Peter in the past I had become frustrated because he plays so slowly. The upshot was that I would end up going for a shot that I would never consider, just to try and make something happen. I would miss and Peter would get in among the balls, make a break and beat me. But this was the final of the World Championship and there was no way I was going to lose by playing stupid shots. He was going to have to work out his own way of beating me because I sure as hell wasn't going to help him. Del and I agreed that, if Peter wanted to be there until 1am, we would be prepared to be there until 4am.

I vowed that I would not lose my patience. I would rather have gone out there and knocked balls in for fun, making umpteen century breaks and bringing the crowd to their feet, but I knew that was never going to happen.

Peter is a friend of mine, bless him, but when he starts to fall behind he becomes even slower, so I just hoped that the crowd in The Crucible had stocked up on Red Bull. I don't know if Peter does it deliberately but things were so slow that we only managed to get 6 of 8 frames played in the first session, after which I led 4-2. I know that I found it painful both to watch and to play in, so goodness knows what the spectators and the millions of fans watching on TV must have thought. Yes, there is an art to safety play but nobody wants to see it drag on. And I include most of the players in that.

The evening session was a killer because we had to catch up on the frames we hadn't completed in the afternoon. It was ghastly. Utter rubbish. But the good news for Dott fans – and there were some – was that, at the end of it all, I was leading 11-5, which meant I 'only' needed to win 7 more frames to become world champion. Mind you, at the rate we were playing them, that could have taken another week to achieve!

There were interminable safety battles but I was winning them and I knew that I had to stick with that tactic. If you beat Peter Ebdon in the safety exchanges, you beat Peter Ebdon. Full stop.

Throughout the match it seemed that every time I got to a break of about 40 I would run out of position. I would have given anything to have turned those 40 breaks into centuries, punctuated by exhibition shots, but it was obvious that I was going to play safe, try to put Peter in trouble and wait for another opportunity to come along. The frames were long, drawn-out affairs and almost all of them were scrappy. As players, we want to entertain the supporters but, at times during that match, I felt like we were keeping them from their beds.

The final is played over two days: the first Sunday and Bank Holiday Monday in May. On the Monday morning I was on the practice table in The Crucible and I could hear the TV link. Clive Everton, Phil Yates and one or two others were talking and they were all saying more or less the same thing: 'I think this will be Peter's big session. This will be where he really digs deep and makes his comeback.' Whether they were saying this for the benefit of the viewers, trying to convince them that it would end up as a nail-biting final, I don't know, but I looked at Del and said, 'There will be no comeback. This match, this final, this Championship is mine and nobody is going to take it away from me.'

I was psyched up and I wanted to finish Peter off in that third session. I knew that, if it had been me and I was 11-5 down, I would believe it was last-chance-saloon time. He had to be feeling the same way.

Once again the speed of play was funereal and we only managed to get through a further 6 frames but I edged it 4-2, exactly as I had planned it, so we were going to be heading into the final session with me leading 15-7 and needing just 3 more frames to make all my dreams come true. As far as I was concerned, it was an unassailable lead. I might even have allowed my thoughts to wander and start to consider what I was going to say in my victory speech. I had to remember to thank all the right people and, whatever I did, not to forget a mention for Elaine and Lewis. And should I mention the snooker clubs where I first played? Perhaps I could have a gentle dig at Mrs McDonald – she would surely be watching.

Wait a minute, Dott. The final wasn't over yet. I was still up against Peter Ebdon. And I suddenly realised that I was completely overwhelmed with exhaustion. I wanted to lie down and go to sleep but there were only about 90 minutes or so between the end of the afternoon session and the beginning of the final session, and I still had to get something to eat. I knew that I had to retain my focus but in the end I had to give in to it, so I had a quick nap. Just go out there and get the job done, I told myself. Maybe he will win a frame or two but we should be able to have an early night.

So the biggest mistake I could possibly have made was to have taken it for granted that the title was already in the bag. I walked back into the arena on that Monday evening in a great mood. Everything was fine until I tried to pot a ball and discovered that my touch had gone. If the pockets had been six inches wide, I would still have struggled to put a ball away.

Suddenly, I could see it all draining away. I had allowed myself to switch off to such an extent that I couldn't get myself going again. How could I have been so bloody stupid? Nobody had told Peter the match was over and I guess he figured that, if he could get a couple of early frames on the board, he might give me something to think about. If I had been capable of gathering my thoughts, he would have been right but I was in a blind panic, thinking about throwing away a certain winning position and being written off in the following day's national press as the biggest choker sport had ever seen.

I had had my foot on his throat and now I had taken it off. It was the most excruciating session of snooker I have ever played and I think I can honestly say that I have never played worse. I could feel the fear welling up in me and I had only negative thoughts, unwise in such a position: Nobody has ever lost from 15-7 up, I thought. This is going to be the most embarrassing defeat in the history of the game. People will be talking about it for years to come.

Whenever I got to the table, I thought only of not making a mistake, rather than looking at a possible pot and convincing myself that I should take it on. I began to worry about what would happen if I missed it. Would I leave Peter the opportunity of a frame-winning break?

So there I was, potting a few balls, then missing to gasps from the crowd, and I would walk back to my chair knowing that everyone there was expecting one of the great sporting collapses. It didn't take long for Ebdon to figure out that I was suffering and, inevitably, his confidence began to grow as quickly as mine was ebbing away; he started playing better than he had at any time during the whole of the final. He was now tucking away balls he had previously been missing and he won the first 4 frames to reduce the deficit to 15-11. Suddenly there was a game on. He knew it. I knew it. Everybody knew it.

At the mid-session interval the TV pundits had a field day, wondering if I would ever pot another ball. They thought I had gone. *I* thought that I had gone. I sat there and felt that I wanted to be sick. Del was trying to get me out of it but I couldn't take in anything he was saying to me. It went in one ear and straight out the other.

I didn't know what I was doing, or even what day of the week it was. When we went back out for the final session I said to myself, Come on, Graeme. Get a grip. Everything is going to be fine. Except that every frame was the same and the sort of thing professional snooker players hate. We would break off and the black would go safe. A safety battle would follow, then the pink would end up safe. And all the reds would be on the side cushion.

And then Ebdon won the next, and the next as well. So now it was 15-13 and it was anybody's game. I say that but I swear to you, at that point, I was wondering how I could possibly win. Every frame was taking 40-odd minutes. Much as I have tried to erase it from my mind, Ebdon even managed to win one marathon frame that lasted well over an hour – a record at the time. Ronnie O'Sullivan has won matches in that time. Good God, so have I. The worst of it was that Ebdon won it on the black. I felt as if somebody had kicked me in the guts. To lose a frame after all the time and effort was just about as bad as it could possibly get.

In the 29th frame I came to the table with the balls situated perfectly. If I couldn't win a frame from this position, I didn't deserve to win the match at all. It was the sort of position I would set up for myself in a practice session, where I would knock the balls straight in. I took a good look around. I couldn't miss but, with each shot I played, I kept thinking, I am going to miss this, I know I am going to miss this. And if I don't, I won't get the position right.

I didn't hit a single shot properly and, as I was making contact with the cue ball, I jumped up, expecting to see the red or the colour rattle in the jaws and stay out. But the balls kept disappearing. My positional play was diabolical so, instead of the easy break it should have been, I had to pot three or four really difficult shots – and before each one the gremlins entered my mind again, telling me I was going to miss.

Fortunately, my cue arm wasn't listening to my brain. I made a 60-odd break and, by some miracle, I managed to win the frame to lead 16-13. I now understood what it meant to fall over the line. Now I only required two more frames. 'Only'? The way I was playing? It was a bit like telling Jean Van De Velde, standing on the final tee at The Open Golf Championship at Carnoustie, that he 'only' needed a six on the par four to become champion. Van De Velde took seven and lost in a playoff. I couldn't afford to take a seven.

In the circumstances, that 60-odd break was one of the best I had ever made but it took an enormous amount out of me and I still required the energy to win two more frames. I wasn't sure I had the energy even to win one more.

Ebdon refused to buckle and came back to win the 30th frame, so now it was 16-14. Finally, all my years of experience were to kick in, thanks to a talking-to I gave myself during a toilet break. Graeme, you're going to have to change something because, if you carry on like this, you're going to come off second best again, and you haven't been through all of this to be runner-up. Whatever you have done to get here is no longer working. Do something different.

I washed my face and splashed some water on my hair. I may even have got some water on my waistcoat. I looked at myself in the mirror and continued with the discussion I was having with myself. You can't wait until it gets to 16-all before trying something different. It might be too late by then. You need to try something right now.

I decided to go out there and play as I had done when I was a teenager. That meant attacking the balls and increasing the tempo. If I am going to lose, I am going to lose while having a go, instead of playing like a lost soul. Armed with an entirely different outlook, I was now faced with a safety shot from Peter. I responded with a safety shot of my own but, instead of glancing off the pack or going for a loose red, I chose to open up the balls so that, if I could get in, there would be a chance to polish off the frame in one visit. If I leave a red, I reasoned, I leave a red.

Peter got in during the 31st frame and he was on 50-odd and looked like he was going to win the frame but I wasn't too bothered. He may be on course to cut back my lead to 16-15 but my new outlook meant that I could snatch and win the next frame.

And then he missed. Up till now, I'd hardly pocketed a ball all night but, fired by adrenalin, I produced a 60-odd break that was the best clearance of my life. I started off with a plant, then potted the brown. I realised there were a couple of reds in the open and kept telling myself that this was good because it was giving me the chance to try out this new high-speed approach to the game. Two more reds and two more colours... All of a sudden it was as if I had spent the previous three hours playing with my hands tied behind my back but now somebody had cut the rope and freed me. There were a couple of tricky shots but I was confident I could get them. I was aware that I was starting to shake – I knew that if I could win this frame, I would be so close to the finishing line.

There was a hard red down the cushion – if I had played the same shot an hour previously, I would have rolled it in slowly, just to make sure that I potted it. This time, I smacked it in, concentrating on getting good position with the cue ball. I wanted to get the white ball cleaned but decided not to because I didn't want to lose the momentum. Next came a pink, then I needed all the colours to win. Missing was not an option but, as I kept going for the balls, they just kept dropping into the pockets. Even though I say so myself, it was a phenomenal clearance. As I completed it, I realised that all my exhaustion had gone. The only part of the final I have ever watched back is that frame-winning clearance.

So I led 17-14 and this time I was certain that I would get the frame I needed for victory. Another toilet break, another chat with myself. Right, you've got away with it. You have endured four hours of torture but you have come out the other side. Go back in there and win the final frame and we can all get out of here.

I potted the final ball at 12.52am, which meant it was the

latest finish in the history of the Championship. I would have preferred to make history for other reasons but, at that moment, I really didn't care. I had done it. I had finally done it. After 12 years as a professional, I had won my first tournament – 18 frames to Peter Ebdon's 14. I was the 2006 world champion.

While I hadn't won by the 18-10 margin that I should have done, I felt an incredible sense of relief that I hadn't thrown it away. Over the two days of the final, I had gone through every emotion in the book and there are some feelings I would never want to experience again. Elaine came down into the arena, gave me the most enormous hug and told me how proud she was of me. I was happy for everybody who had helped and supported me, especially my mentor Alex.

As a little boy I had dreamed of becoming world champion and now I had done it. Those dreams would also have included newspaper headlines hailing me as a hero but the reality was somewhat different: the press reports were more interested in slaughtering Peter and I for what they felt was one of the worst finals anybody could remember. Some of what was written was vile. There was no interest in the fact that I had become world champion or that I had trounced Ronnie O'Sullivan. As far as they were concerned, it was boring and the standard of play was really poor. I was even described by some as one of the worst world champions of all time – and I didn't deserve that.

I have been quite vocal about this but I came out and said that, in my opinion, it was unreasonable to expect two players to compete in best-of-31-frame semi-finals, to be followed over the next 2 days by a best-of-35-frame final. There are all sorts of reasons why this is not fair. One player may win with a session to spare, while the other finalist may find himself involved in a marathon, which could run till late on the Saturday night, but would still have to face the biggest match of his life the next day.

I am convinced that, if you allowed both finalists a chance to get some rest, you would end up with a much better final. Would it really be too much to give the finalists a day off? You could either declare an official rest day or you could stage a series of exhibition matches, perhaps the women's final, some seniors' games or a junior Pot Black-style competition. There may even be some merit in a third and fourth place playoff, just as they have at football's World Cup. The losing semi-finalists could play a best-of-19-frame match that would give the fans another match.

Furthermore, why can't we have the afternoon sessions starting at, say, midday? Television dictates everything that happens. If the afternoon session does not kick off until 3pm, is it any great surprise that sometimes the players don't manage to get through the full eight frames before they have to be taken off before the evening session gets under way? In the early rounds you could find yourself playing a session at 10am and when it finishes you don't come back to the arena until 7pm, which means you get a chance to have a proper break. And we often have an afternoon session one day, get the night off and come back the following morning.

Nottingham player Anthony Hamilton told me that he could never win the World Championship and it had nothing to do with his ability. He said, 'Graeme, I have played quarter-finals at The Crucible and I have been dead on my feet because of all the concentration that is required, so I cannot even begin to imagine how anybody copes with a marathon semi followed by a final.' Things have changed though. Back in the 1970s and 1980s, the top players would get an easy ride in the first couple of rounds but the quality of snooker has improved; the standards are much higher and you have to be at your best right from the start.

Subsequent finals have lasted longer and finished even later than ours. I hate to say 'I told you so', but I did. All the players feel the same way and something has to change. It has been suggested that time limits could be introduced on every shot. It would not bother me if that happened but I can't see it and it would not solve the problem anyway. If a player was caught in two minds between a safety and going for a pot and he knew that he was under time pressure, he would definitely go for the safety. There are too many slow players in the game and something needs to be done but I am just not convinced that is the answer.

Back at my triumph at the 2006 World Championship, I told the press that it wasn't our intention to put on a bad final. There was just a whole series of frames where the black went safe. When that happens it's always scrappy. Even the Scottish press, happy enough that a home-grown player had won, could not resist having a dig by pointing out that my highest break in the final was 69. I held my hands up and admitted that I had played rubbish, because I didn't want anybody getting the idea that this was how I normally played. And surely, if they had watched my game against Ronnie, they would have realised that I had something to offer and that I was actually a pretty worthy world champion. Did they want me to hand the title back? I wasn't there to entertain the press. I was there to win. If I had got frustrated, gone for shots and lost, Peter would have won and he wouldn't have felt bad about it, so why should I have done?

I respect the commentator and writer Clive Everton, who has an encyclopaedic knowledge of snooker, although I was incredibly disappointed by something he said later. It was during some documentary about Ronnie O'Sullivan, where various people were paying tribute to him. Up popped Clive talking about that 2006 semi-final at The Crucible and he said it was more a case of Ronnie losing than me beating him. I thought it was an astonishing thing for him to say and it probably hurt me more coming from him because I like and respect the man. 'Everybody's the same,' I said with a sigh. 'Nobody sees it from the other point of view. Why can't he just give me credit for a job well done?'

Ronnie has beaten me lots of times and I am the first to admit that he is in a different class. I can accept it when I lose to a better player but, when I beat him in that semi-final, I was in a different class, not him. He lost because I was the better player and it wouldn't have hurt Clive to have acknowledged that. If he couldn't have done that, he just shouldn't have mentioned that match. Yes, Ronnie ended up in one of his moods but it was because I kept him away from the table – and that is the only way you can beat Ronnie O'Sullivan.

My life was a whirl after my victory at The Crucible. My prize was a cheque for £200,000 and I wanted to do something to help secure the future for my wife and family. I couldn't imagine a better way of doing that than being able to say that we owned our house so one of the first things I did was pay off our mortgage. I knew it was the right thing to do, even though it cost me almost every penny of the prize money.

Some people might have gone out and bought a flash sports car. I have got a nice car – a Porsche Cayenne 4x4 – but I bought it because it is a good family car, not because it has a Porsche badge on the bonnet. And I fret about the price of petrol just as much as the next man does – my car does about 20 miles per gallon and, with petrol the price it is, I sometimes feel like I am taking out a second mortgage each time I fill it up.

My best friend Jim Fisher was with me the day I bought the Porsche. It is not in my nature to buy the first thing I see and I knew that this was a car that was going to cost a fair amount of money, so I spent some time looking for one at the right price. Eventually I tracked one down to a garage in Aberdeen. As we drove away from the garage in the new vehicle, we encountered some roadworks but I was certain that we were on a dual carriageway. I overtook a car and was chatting away to Jim without a care in the world, when suddenly I heard him screaming at me, 'Pull the car in! Pull the bloody car in – there's a car coming!' With that, he went to grab the wheel. I suddenly realised that I was on the wrong side of the road and just about managed to get the car back into the right lane. It would have gone down as the fastest accident in the history of motoring – I'd only owned the Porsche about two minutes.

Among the messages of goodwill I received during that World Championship was a telegram from Alex McLeish, the Rangers manager at the time. The message arrived during my semi-final to tell me that I was doing really well, and that all the players and everybody at Glasgow Rangers Football Club were rooting for me. It meant something special to me because it was something that Alex didn't need to do. As you can imagine, my dad – another Rangers fan – was thrilled when he saw it.

When John Higgins had won the World Championship he took the trophy to Celtic Park and paraded it before the fans. I thought that, if I won, I would love to do the same thing at Ibrox. I have a friend who has a box at the ground and he was instrumental in arranging it. As I approached the entrance there was somebody waiting for me to remove the green and white 888.com ribbons and replace them with the red, white and blue colours of Rangers.

As I walked down the tunnel my stomach started to churn. How would the fans react to me? Did they care about the fact that one of their supporters had won the World Snooker Championship? What would happen if they booed me? It occurred to me that I might walk out onto the pitch and there might be silence. How would I feel if they didn't even clap? Every Rangers fan knows that I support the team and that I go to games whenever I can so at least they would know that I wasn't jumping on some kind of bandwagon.

In the event, it was an amazing experience. We were playing Hearts, the ground was packed and they gave me a tremendous cheer. It was another career highlight and a moment that will stay with me until the day I die. I looked around the ground and realised that many of the fans were waving banners with my name on them. So not only did they know I was coming but they went out of their way to make it extra special for me.

And it got even better. The Hearts supporters started chanting, 'One Stephen Hendry, there's only one Stephen Hendry.' Needless to say, the Rangers fans weren't going to stand for that and immediately hit back with, 'One Graeme Dott, there's only one Graeme Dott.' It was an unbelievable moment to hear 40,000 people singing my name. I later received a DVD and have since shown it to my son, Lewis. Even now, it makes the hairs on the back of my neck stand on end just to think about it.

Alex was ill so I effectively had no manager but the phone was ringing non-stop with people wanting me to do this, that and the other, and I hadn't the first idea what to do. Did I say yes to everything and try to make as much money as possible, or did I pick and choose? There was one month where I was committed to doing something every single day. There were radio and TV interviews, an appearance on a football phone-in show... it went on and on.

I also did *A Question of Sport*, which was great fun and was one of the few things I got paid for doing. Ally McCoist, the former Rangers player and an idol of mine, was my team captain and he was a scream. And there was Jason White, the Scottish rugby-union flanker, who is a giant of a man, as big as I am small. Elaine went to London with me and it was a great day out. Ally knew that I was a Rangers fan and made a big fuss of me. And I even got my question right or, rather, McCoist whispered the answer to me. There had been two overseas players at The Crucible that year – one was James Wattana and I had to name the other. It was Marco Fu.

I received other requests. Some people I knew, although not terribly well, would ask me to attend events to present some prizes. For instance, I would be asked to attend a charity golf day and I would agree to play. These things were no great hardship and I am not suggesting that I should have been paid for taking part in a charity event but it all begins to mount up. A manager would have ensured that I prioritised and that I had some time for myself and for my family.

I kept thinking that, although I was world snooker champion, I didn't want to come across in a way where people would look at me and get the impression that I thought I was too good for them. So I guess that I went the other way and agreed to do far too much. If you have a golf day on the Monday, radio on the Tuesday, a TV interview on the Wednesday, time with a journalist on the Thursday for a newspaper article, a prize-giving on the Friday, you end up going round and round in circles. The days began to merge into one and it was non-stop but I was the world champion and that was the thought that drove me on.

I also found that I was answering the same questions, over and over again. I have always enjoyed my privacy but, now, everywhere I went, there would be somebody who would recognise me. In particular, I lost count of the number of people who would come up to me and say, 'Aye, you kept me up late the night you won the World Championship, Graeme.' You have to laugh and make out that nobody has ever said that to you before but it eventually becomes pretty trying. Even Elaine kept being told by everyone she met about how late they got to bed that night.

Day after day, wherever I went, everyone would want me to bring the trophy with me and ask me to have a picture taken with them. There would always be calls for 'just one more photo', which would prompt yet more people into asking if they could also have a picture. And then the next day I would have to do the same thing all over again.

Despite my new champion status and the busy life it brought me, there were not huge sums of money rolling into my bank account, that's for sure. Maybe it would have been different if I'd had a manager. I wouldn't have swapped it for anything though.

CHAPTER SIXTEEN

THE FADING OF THE LIGHT

*I*know that many of you will wonder why my manager and father-in-law Alex was not at my side when I won the World Championship. He wasn't there because he was extremely sick at the time. His illness would have a devastating effect upon me and the people I loved and cared about. Even now, I still look back on what he had to go through and it breaks my heart.

Alex had always been there for me, so full of life, so confident that I would make it to the very top of professional snooker. His presence in my life and the presence of his family in mine meant everything to me. I believe that Alex would have done anything for me. He never once asked for anything from me, other than to believe in myself.

We first became aware that all was not well towards the end of 2005. Elaine pointed out that her father had lost weight but we put that down to the fact that, since his wife, May, had

155

died, he had let himself go a little and hadn't been eating properly. He came to our house to celebrate Christmas and we were aware that he only picked at his dinner. After he had gone home, Elaine said she was sure he wasn't well, but I suppose that I just dismissed it as one of those things. This was Alex. He would be fine.

I got a phone call from him on 13 January 2006 to say that he wasn't feeling well. I went to visit him and, when I arrived at his house, it was obvious that he was in a great deal of pain. He hadn't told anybody about his condition but he confided in me that every time he went to the toilet he was peeing blood. This had been going on for weeks, perhaps longer. Mortified, I told him that he had to go and see his doctor immediately. In fact, I insisted that I was going to take him to the hospital and phoned Elaine to tell her.

For all that Alex was a big bloke, he was a typical man. He didn't want any fuss and I guess that, like the rest of us, he just crossed his fingers, hoped for the best and trusted that his illness would just go away. In truth, I am certain that he was also scared of what the doctor might tell him but he had done himself no favours in leaving it.

'You have no choice, Alex,' I told him. 'Peeing blood is not normal. There must be something wrong so get an appointment made and just go to see the doctor.'

It was unusual for me to be telling him what to do and he wasn't keen: 'I don't want to see a doctor, Graeme,' he replied.

'Don't be daft. Get an appointment or else we can go to the hospital right now. I will take you.'

Eventually he agreed to let me take him to the hospital. On arrival, he was in quite a state and unable to pass urine. By the time Elaine joined us, he was delirious – he felt like his insides were going to burst and insisted that we get him a doctor. They put a catheter in him, which helped to relieve some of the discomfort, but the colour soon drained from Elaine's face when she realised that the catheter bag had filled with blood. Though this didn't really register with me, Elaine later told me that she hadn't wanted to share her anxiety with me because I was making lots of optimistic noises. To be honest, in my naivety, I was convinced that everything was going to be all right. As the hospital kept Alex in overnight, we returned home. During our journey, I told Elaine that I was sure that her father had kidney stones. Where that thought came from I don't know but I convinced myself I was right.

When we went back to see Alex the next day, it was perfectly obvious that he didn't want to be there. He had been subjected to a series of tests and scans, and there was something near his right kidney that they wanted to investigate further, so the doctors would have to carry out further tests. Alex didn't want to know. He was told he would have to have a CT scan.

It always seemed that, when bad news had to be broken at home, I was away. Alex was due to get his results while I was playing in The Masters at Wembley in 2006 and, during my absence, he was told that they had discovered a tumour. I was oblivious to it all. Maybe I didn't want to face up to any of the possibilities so I made up my mind that, whatever was wrong with him, they would be able to put it right, and tried to forget that he had told me of passing blood for several weeks. Elaine phoned me to confirm that it was kidney stones after all and there was, indeed, nothing to worry about. I knew it – everything was going to be all right after all. I knew it.

I was duly knocked out of The Masters and headed for home but Elaine phoned me and asked me to meet her at Berries, the hotel Alex owned. I remember wondering why Elaine would be there. After a long drive back from London I got to the hotel, parked the car and went inside, and the moment I walked into the room I knew that something wasn't right. The whole family were there. They had been given the results of the CT scan. It was Alex who told me the shattering news. 'Graeme, we didn't want to worry you while you were playing snooker but I've got cancer.'

It was like being punched in the jaw. I could hear what he had just told me but I wasn't listening because this was big Alex Lambie and he was indestructible. He couldn't possibly have cancer. But he did and it had spread from his kidney into his chest wall and into his lungs. Then came the knockout punch, the one that put me on the floor: 'I've got a year to live, son.'

I could not believe what I was hearing. I ran outside and all I could hear were the words 'I've got a year to live'. He had kidney cancer and it was inoperable. Who knows what they would have been able to do for him had he gone to them at the first sign that something wasn't right? But he hadn't and now the clock was ticking. This man who had done so much for me was living on borrowed time and there was nothing that Alex Junior, Elaine or Graeme Dott could do about it.

That night, we all sat around talking and cuddling each other. It's funny but in those sorts of situations, people always end up talking about the old days, and that's what we did. We recalled happier times and, briefly at least, it made us all feel a little bit better.

I felt incredibly guilty that I hadn't been around while Elaine, her sister Pauline and Alex Junior had to sit with their father as a doctor told him that he had cancer and was going to die. Pauline had run out of the room and Elaine, her brother and her father sat and hugged each other, all three of them crying as they realised the enormity of what they had been told.

I mentioned just now that awful things tended to happen to the people I love when I was away playing snooker and it began with the death of Alex's wife, May, in the spring of 2002. I was set to play in the World Championship at The Crucible and she had been diagnosed shortly before the tournament began. Elaine and Alex insisted that I went ahead and played, and I won my match. But my massive high was short lived when Elaine phoned. 'Graeme, my mum's died.' How was it possible? She was only 43. Nobody had given us any clue that she had so little time left.

I left Sheffield straight away. May's funeral was horrendous and, when it was over, I had to go back to The Crucible and somehow try to concentrate on playing snooker. It meant nothing to me. My head was all over the place and I felt empty inside so it was little wonder that I lost 13-2 to John Higgins.

Alex and May had been soul mates and he was never the same man after her passing. It might have been easier if he'd had longer to prepare himself for it. He used to spend a great deal of time at the cemetery. I guess he found some comfort in going down there and talking to May but it was as if a part of him died along with her.

I hated seeing him ill but it did give me an opportunity to give him something back. For the first time, I could be there for him. He accepted that he had cancer and, at the same time, I believe he also accepted that it was going to beat him. For all that he made defiant noises, I never had the feeling that he was fighting it in the way that Paul Hunter had. Paul announced to the world that he would fight his cancer with his dying breath but Alex was different and it upset me terribly.

Living with somebody who has cancer is horrific because it is not just the victim who suffers. Everybody else in the family goes through it too and there is nothing more soul destroying than watching somebody you love fade away. Cancer is an evil condition because it shows no mercy.

We tried to keep Alex's spirits up and sometimes he still had good days. Obviously, his involvement with my snooker career all but came to an end and that was incredibly difficult to cope with because he had always been there for me. We were a team and we had been everywhere together. This, remember, was a man who would watch me play a qualifying match in Blackpool and would then drive home to Larkhall to see to business, before setting off at the crack of dawn the following day to drive straight back to Blackpool. Being without him was like losing my right arm.

I was still playing and, unbelievably, I was playing very well, considering all the worries in my head, but Alex had made it abundantly clear to me that he wanted life to go on as normal for everybody else. I would turn up for tournaments and people would ask where he was but the conversations always ended pretty quickly when I would tell them he had cancer. And the thing is that, when people learn that somebody has cancer, they tend not to ask again because they know that the only way is down.

It was hard to play while Alex was suffering but it was also easier being away from home than it was to see the pain he was in. Elaine was also going through a dreadful time watching her father fade away in front of her eyes. While I was playing snooker I was able to blank everything out and, the better I played, the longer I was at tournament venues, which meant I did not have to come home and face reality. It sounds incredibly selfish but it is really not meant to be.

Alex took it particularly hard that he wasn't by my side throughout the 2006 World Championship. Sitting at home watching me win my first two matches, he told Elaine that he really wanted to go to Sheffield to see me play, so she asked the specialist if it would be possible. The doctor realised not only that I was doing well but also that it might be Alex's last chance to see me play in a major tournament, so he gave the OK. His brother, Jack, drove him down to Sheffield, where they took a room together at the city's Hilton Hotel. It was a brief respite for Alex, a few days when he was able to try and forget about his illness, mix with the snooker players and drink in the atmosphere of The Crucible. All those years before, this was what he had dreamed about for me.

When I won the World Championship the thing that pleased me most of all was that he had seen me do it. It meant everything to me when, at the end, he came out into the arena in front of everybody and – with Elaine looking on – hugged the life out of me. It was one of the best moments of my life and also one of the saddest because I knew that Alex and I would never be in this position again.

I now feel that I won that title more for Alex Lambie than I did for myself. Had I not been world champion, I might well have taken time away from snooker but Alex would never have allowed me. His view was that I had a duty to go out and compete, and prove to everybody that I was a worthy champion. I played for Alex as much as I played for myself because I knew that every victory, every century break would give him something to smile about and just might help him to take his mind off his illness, even if it were only for a few moments.

There were moments of optimism too, when the doctors would try different drugs and he would respond and seem to get a bit brighter. It never lasted, of course, but with cancer hope is everything. You pray every day that a miracle will happen; that they will tell you they made a mistake. We seemed to spend our lives clutching at straws.

But some of the drugs had the opposite effect. There were times when he could barely stand up and was unable to walk. Eventually he was advised to have his kidney removed. The doctor told him that it would improve his quality of life and give him a little longer so we encouraged him. He hadn't done anything to the house after May died so, when he was in hospital for an operation, we decided to redecorate the place and we really enjoyed ourselves. It gave us something to focus on. He went to stay with his sister for six weeks while he recovered and, when he walked into his home for the first time, he stopped and said, 'I knew you lot had done this.' It turned out that he had spotted paint in our hair when we'd been visiting him in hospital. We had also dumped a lot of his old furniture so it was like him coming back to a brand-new home. It was a rare moment of light relief.

That operation gave Alex an additional five months but the day they took his kidney out was the day that all hope was extinguished. From that moment on he was a very sick man. He would come up to see us but I always felt that he couldn't wait to go home and climb back into his bed. It was no way to live. We would go and visit him and he would be asleep on the sofa.

Pauline was with Alex one day when the doctor took her to one side to tell her that the cancer had spread to his other kidney and to his liver. Elaine told her brother and sister that she wanted to break the news to her father because she didn't think she could carry that information around with her and still be able to look her dad in the eye. And so the three of them took the decision to tell their father and he was like a little boy. 'No, no, please, no. I want to beat this.'

Alex, his son and I sat and hugged and bawled our eyes out, praying for a miracle that we knew would never come.

On 25 November 2006 we went down to have dinner with Alex and we took Lewis with us. Elaine gave her father a tiny portion of chicken but he couldn't eat it and went through to the living room to sit down in front of the TV, followed by Lewis, who cuddled up to his grandfather on the sofa. Elaine had recently bought a camera and went to take a photo of the two of them; Alex told her not to because he wasn't feeling up to it but she took it anyway. It would be the last photo she would ever take of her father.

Later that night Pauline phoned to tell Elaine that she had to come to the house because Alex's temperature was sky high, his pulse was racing and his blood pressure was very low. Elaine called NHS-24 and they arranged for a doctor to come out and see him – a locum who didn't know him. His suggestion was to cover Alex with a blanket. It was a waste of everybody's time.

The next day, Alex was taken back into hospital. And now we knew that the end was near. There were difficult issues to be addressed in terms of his ongoing care and it fell to Elaine to tell the doctor who was looking after him that Alex's comfort was the most important thing for all of us. None of us wanted him to suffer. We were asked whether we wanted Alex to be resuscitated if he suffered heart failure. How can any family be expected to answer such a question dispassionately? We told the doctors that, no, we did not want him to be resuscitated. If it came to that, he had suffered enough.

Jim Fisher, my best friend, was a rock throughout this period. He is a self-employed plumber but he accompanied me to tournaments and did his best to keep my spirits up. He had lost his parents so he knew what I was going through.

My biggest difficulty was that I bottled everything up and that would cause me real problems further down the road. I think it is a typical male characteristic. Most men prefer to be the strong, silent type, failing to recognise that owning up to your true feelings and discussing them with your loved ones can actually be incredibly cathartic. I found it easier to go to tournaments and think of nothing.

In December 2006 I was due to play in the UK Championship at York. I packed my clothes and, before heading south of the border, headed for the hospital to check in on Alex. He looked awful. Elaine was there too and there was very little said between the three of us. I knew he was in dreadful pain and I just wished there was something I could do to help ease his suffering. I sat with him for about 20 minutes and then told him I was travelling down to York. He still knew what tournament I was playing in. Elaine left the ward to speak to a nurse and Alex lifted his mask, grabbed my hand and squeezed it hard.

'Just show everybody how good you are, Graeme,' he whispered and he tried to smile.

I am convinced that he knew it would be the last time I would see him alive. I told him that I would see him when I got back but, deep down, I knew that this was our final moment together. I left the hospital, got in the car and didn't stop crying for 30 minutes. Poor Jim was with me and I don't think he knew what to say. Sometimes, silence speaks volumes.

We got to York and, by the time we arrived, I had blanked everything out again. I was able to forget about it all for a few days. It would soon all catch up with me but, for now, I played brilliantly in the UK Championship, only losing to Stephen Hendry in the semi-finals. It was almost as if Alex was providing an unseen hand on the tiller. I led Hendry 7-5 and was desperate to beat him, reach the final and win the tournament for Alex but it wasn't to be and he fought back to win 9-7. It was a quality match; the sort of game that was a privilege to be involved in.

Afterwards, I phoned Elaine to tell her that I had lost. She didn't say very much, only that she was looking forward to me returning home. Then she called me back to tell me that Alex had died at 2.05pm on 16 December 2006. He was just 58. He took his last breath with his immediate family at his bedside. I felt as if my world had come to an end. He was far too young to die. When I got home, Elaine and I collapsed into each other's arms.

I tried to cope by not doing anything about it, whereas I should have faced up to my emotions. I couldn't accept that he was gone so I pretended it hadn't happened. And increasingly I found myself looking forward to the next tournament on the schedule because that was another opportunity for me to escape from it all. I was reminded of Alex's death every day because Elaine was trying to deal with it too, trying to come to terms with the loss of her second parent before she had reached the age of 30. Nobody should have to go through something like that.

Apart from anything else, I was angry that Alex had not been given the opportunity to enjoy plenty of quality time with Lewis. It seemed so unfair. I wanted my son to know what a wonderful man his grandfather was and now he would not be able to experience that for himself. We could tell him the stories about Alex, of course, but it was hardly the same thing. I battled to revive Elaine's spirits but, all the while, I was neglecting my own feelings – neglect that would have its own consequences.

CHAPTER SEVENTEEN

DOTT, YOU'VE GOT A PROBLEM

I was at The Masters in January 2007 when I got a phone call from Elaine, who was pregnant at the time. She was training to become a nurse and the pregnancy was unplanned but we both thought that it might be a blessing after Alex's recent passing. Lewis was going to have a brother or a sister.

Elaine didn't know how far gone she was so she went with her best friend Stacy for a routine scan but sensed that there was something wrong. She asked the doctor if everything was all right, figuring that, at worst, she could have miscarried without knowing it. The baby was fine but the doctor told Elaine that he had found cysts in her ovaries, before adding, 'I don't know if they are benign or cancerous.' The thought hadn't entered her head until he put it there. She would have to go for tests.

Not surprisingly, Elaine was beside herself. Her mum and dad had both died of cancer and she was now convinced that she had it too. The next day she had to return to the hospital for a series of blood tests and biopsies, convinced that, when all the results came back, she would be told that she had ovarian cancer. Another tournament, more bad news and, once again, I wasn't there to support my wife. I remember thinking, What have we done to deserve this? Can anything else go wrong in our lives? Why me? Why us?

I had cried on the phone when Elaine broke the news to me and I continued to sob after our conversation. I didn't know what to do. I came to the conclusion that, if I played the match, I would not be that much later in getting home, so that's what I decided to do. People had paid to come and see me and I'd have needed a reason for withdrawing from the tournament. I couldn't face that.

I tried to say all the right things to Elaine but, deep down, I feared the worst too. I had made up my mind that she was almost certainly suffering from cancer and I was already making plans to take a year out in order to look after her and Lewis. I wanted to go home right there and then. The only reason that I didn't was because I was world champion and felt that I would let the crowds down if I pulled out of competitions. But in truth, I knew that, in such stressful circumstances, the chances of me winning any matches were slim at best and, indeed, I lost in the second round of The Masters to Stephen Lee.

I knew that Elaine would get her results a couple of days later so I told the media that I might not be back in the game for a while. They wanted to know why but I knew that I had already said too much and, before I knew it, news of her cancer scare had been leaked and was all over the papers. To this day I still don't know how they found out.

I headed home with a horrible feeling in the pit of my stomach. Life couldn't get much worse but I knew that I had to be strong for Elaine. The days before we got the results of the tests were among the longest of my life but, thankfully, we found out soon afterwards that the cysts were not cancerous and that Elaine was fine. I was thrilled. It should have been the start of a happy chapter in our lives but whoever it is that governs these things had decided he wasn't quite finished with us.

When Elaine had to return to hospital a month later for a further scan, I was away at yet another tournament, this time at the Wales Open. Because of the cysts, they'd decided that they wanted to keep a close eye on her and she was told that there was no longer a baby. This time she didn't even have Stacy with her and she then had to face the prospect of having the foetus removed. It was another phone call that broke my heart but at least I knew that she was all right.

After everything else the two of us had been through, we dealt with this latest devastating news pretty well. She had not been too far down the road with the pregnancy, thank God. I recovered from the news relatively quickly, although I am sure it affected Elaine more deeply. The good news was that the doctors told us there was no reason why we could not try for another baby.

My friend Jim Fisher was brilliant and supportive. He took Elaine to the hospital, waited for her while she had the procedure, which is effectively an abortion, then took her home. I phoned her and tried to reassure her that we could try for another baby whenever she felt that the time was right. I cannot imagine a worse ordeal for a woman. One minute she was pregnant, the next she wasn't. Young Lewis didn't know it at the time but he helped her through it just by being there. It took time to heal and she was especially low at around the time the baby would have been born. It is hardly surprising that Elaine was on the verge of a nervous breakdown but at least she was able to confide in a therapist, who helped her get through it all.

As if all this wasn't enough, my mum had also fallen very ill. She made an appointment to go and see the doctor but, as she was walking to the surgery, she began to feel even worse. Somehow she managed to complete her journey there, where the doctor told her that he was certain she was having a heart attack. Naturally, they rushed her to hospital and conducted a series of tests. It soon became obvious that her arteries were blocked and surgery was the only option. The doctors were brilliant and Mum had a triple-heart-bypass operation, after which she made a full recovery.

It seemed that every person I cared about was suffering. I suppose it was inevitable that it would eventually have an impact on me. If only Elaine had known what I was going through. But I was pretending that everything was fine. I spent most of my life walking around in a daze. I felt nothing. It's a funny thing but, when somebody who is close to you dies, people will come up to you for a short time afterwards and tell you how sorry they are to hear the news and then they never mention it again. When you are the central character, it is with you all the time. In my head, Alex was still around. I couldn't accept that he was dead and quickly found myself in a spiral of despair.

Away from the snooker table I didn't want to do anything.

I didn't want to talk to Elaine and I didn't really want to talk to anybody else. Lewis kept me going and I was still happy to play with him; in fact, I probably spent even more time with him because he was little more than a baby and I knew that he would not ask me any difficult questions.

Your children just want your time and your love, and it was easy to give him both. I must have been impossible to live with from Elaine's point of view though. Thank goodness she has the patience of a saint. There were times when we would go out for a meal and I would sit there and hardly say a word to her all night long.

Throughout my life people have always said, 'Cheer up, Graeme. It might never happen.' Some people look happy but I am afraid that I have always been somebody who looks downbeat. There is little doubt in my mind that I had slipped into a pretty deep depression very soon after Alex's death but I didn't realise it at the time. I have always been a deep thinker but this was something else.

Eventually I knew that I couldn't carry on the way I was so I made an appointment to see a therapist, who quickly concluded that my problems had been brought on by the fact that I had not allowed myself the time to grieve. Elaine and Alex Junior had gone through the natural process of grief and, while it wasn't easy for either of them, they did, at least, come to terms with the loss of Alex. Until I was able to face up to it and accept what had happened, I could not do that. I had been escaping my true feelings by going to one tournament or another, locking away all emotions so that I wouldn't need to think about Alex. It was only when I came off the table that I had to face reality again – except that I wouldn't.

I look back on that time now and honestly cannot believe how consistently well I played. I was vying with Ken Doherty and John Higgins to finish 2007 as the world No. 1 but anybody who watched me play would never have guessed that there was anything wrong. People who did not know me must have thought that I had taken the death of Alex really well but I was basically just lying to everybody by giving them the impression that everything was all right.

I have never been a person who is prepared to show emotion in public, although the tears have never been far away as I have relived Alex's passing for this book. You may think that you are over something but, when you talk and write about it, suddenly you realise that those feelings are all still very, very raw.

CHAPTER EIGHTEEN

MADE IN CHINA 2007

*T*he two worst matches I have played at The Crucible have both been against Ian McCulloch. He had already beaten me 10-9 in the first round in 2004. Three years later, when I returned to Sheffield to defend my title, he was again my first-round opponent. I had the chance to finish the 2006/07 season as the world No. 1, which would have been an amazing thing for me to achieve, especially with everything that was going on in my head away from the table.

I don't like playing McCulloch. The top and bottom of it is that he is far too slow for my liking. He always looks again at the same shot before he takes it. The worst thing is that, because you are involved in the match with him, you end up being tarred with the same brush. It drives me mad and, if I was a spectator, I wouldn't want to watch it. I'd say that McCulloch has been better when he has played more quickly. At the end of the day, though, it is up to the referee. He can take players to one side and 'advise' them to speed up but when was the last time you saw that happen?

I was happy enough, though, to draw him for a second time at The Crucible. He had beaten me before so now was a good chance to get my revenge and I was a much better player. I regarded him as an easy draw. I'd had a really good season, having reached the semi-finals of the UK Championship and a host of quarter-finals. And just a few weeks before facing him in Sheffield, I had won the 2007 China Open.

Snooker players are treated like gods in China. The opening ceremony of the China Open is shown live on television. We are driven to the arena two at a time and are filmed getting out the car and walking along a red carpet leading into the arena. It's like a Hollywood film premiere or the Oscars. We would also be given cuddly toys – usually teddy bears – to throw to the crowd, then we sign a big board. It is as if we are visiting royalty. I must admit, though, that I find it quite embarrassing that millions of people should look up to me just because I was born with an ability to put a ball in a pocket.

I felt the tournament owed me something because of my dreadful experience getting to China five years earlier and, on this occasion, everything felt just right. My first match was against James Wattana, who had a huge amount of local support, but I came out on top 5-2. In the second round my opponent was Neil Robertson but I hardly drew breath as I beat the Australian 5-1. In the quarter-finals I played John Higgins and I produced some of the best snooker of my life. He won the first 2 frames but I clawed one back and then produced breaks of 84, 97, 106 and 102 to beat him 5-2. I was on cloud nine.

Next to beat, in the semi-final, was Ronnie O'Sullivan and, before the match, I told the press that I hoped he played well when we met. 'I am playing great snooker,' I said, 'and I hope that he is too – because then, if I beat him, you will not be able to slaughter him and, if he beats me, you will not be able to have a go at me either.' I was in control right from the start, winning the opening frame thanks to a 78. Ronnie rolled in a 65 in frame 2 but I still managed to pinch it and, when I took the third and fourth, I knew that there was no way back for him. I eventually beat him 6-2, with breaks of 117 and 99.

My opponent in the final was Jamie Cope, who I had never played before. I won 6 of the 8 frames in the first session to lead 6-2 in the best-of-17-frame match, thanks to breaks of 72, 60, 70 and 95. It meant I only required three more frames for my second tournament victory. Jamie gave me the fright of my life in the evening session when he won the first 3 frames but I was in a really good place on the table and won the frames I required with breaks of 124, 120 and 64. I was the China Open champion and the provisional world No. 1.

After my win I spent a week in China doing a series of exhibition matches – well, I was the world champion after all and it turned out to be a thoroughly enjoyable experience. I visited three or four different cities, although my luggage didn't turn up and nor did my cue, so I was taken to a giant shopping mall where the organisers got me all kitted out and I had to use a borrowed cue.

I also visited Mongolia, where I played a few frames against some locals. Afterwards I was expected to sign some autographs. With fans in Britain, you sign as many autographs as you can while the queue of people waits patiently but, in that part of the world, they come heading towards you like a stampeding herd of cattle. It's extremely intimidating and more than a little bit scary.

I was in the middle of signing autographs when one of the translators I was with informed me that it was time to go. I didn't want to walk away while there were still people waiting so I tried to carry on signing as many autographs as I could. As I was finally taken to the car for the journey back to the hotel, a group of fans followed us, still determined to get my autograph. But while I was happy to continue, my entourage of minders was more reluctant and, before I knew it, they were getting ready to fight the fans. The minders grabbed hold of me, forced me to run into the hotel and pushed me into the lift. My room was on the 12th floor but I was taken to the 20th floor as the translator explained, 'We're taking you to my room in case they know where your room is.' I was kept there for 15 minutes before I could return to my room... all because one of my minders had decided that I had signed enough autographs for one day.

It was quite bizarre to realise that all these people knew who I was. China is a massive growth area for snooker and we keep hearing that there are likely to be more tournaments played there. There was even talk about the World Championship being taken out there but I can't believe that will ever happen. The whole world knows that the Chinese economy is booming and that the place is awash with cash and, that being the case, I do wonder why they don't put up more prize money.

In my view, though, China gets its tournaments on the cheap. I am the first to admit that the Chinese look after us while we are in their country but it is only through collecting prize money that we are able to make a living and it seems to me that the Chinese could afford to stage a few big-money events – the sort that pays the winner £100,000. If the Chinese can't attract sponsors, nobody can.

The Chinese stage two tournaments at present – one in Beijing, the other in Shanghai – and they are as different as chalk and cheese. I prefer the cooler climate in Beijing, whereas the oppressive humidity of Shanghai has an effect on the way the tables play – high humidity makes the cloth run slow and you get all sorts of strange kicks.

The three weeks I spent in China took a huge amount out of me and I hadn't fully recovered by the time I arrived back in England. I had about ten days before the World Championships got under way but my decision to practise non-stop was a mistake. My game was in such good shape and I had won so many tournaments that season that I could have afforded a week off. In addition, because I was back in Sheffield as the defending champion, I had to spend a full day with various media outlets just two days before the competition began. It is exhausting and it takes you away from the things on which you should be concentrating.

So I may have been world champion and winner of the China Open but, as early on as two-all in my first-round match against McCulloch at The Crucible, the alarm bells were starting to ring. There was nothing there, nothing to draw on and, embarrassingly, it seemed that the harder I tried, the worse I got. Plus, of course, there was the matter of how slowly my opponent was playing. I tried to ask the referee to quicken McCulloch's pace but he didn't agree with me that

McCulloch was playing too slowly. Inevitably, I lost the match and, with it, the opportunity to finish the season as world No. 1. I was devastated and decided to get back home as quickly as I possibly could.

In the next round McCulloch went on to play Anthony Hamilton, against whom he lost 13-8. McCulloch was asked a question by one reporter that went something like this: 'After beating the world champion, did you not think you would have had an easier match against Anthony Hamilton?' His reply was that he found it harder to beat Anthony than it was to beat me. I discovered the story while glancing through the sports headlines on Ceefax. I was already in a pretty poor frame of mind but that tipped me over the edge. I thought, I've won the World Championship and the China Open – what's he won? The cause of my anger had nothing to do with the comparison with Anthony – he is a great player – as it would not have mattered which player he had named.

The season was at an end but my annoyance over the episode continued to fester away all summer and, when the next season began in October 2007 with the Grand Prix in Aberdeen, I was asked in one interview about my World Championship defeat. I couldn't help myself: 'For somebody like Ian McCulloch, who has never done anything in snooker and who never will do anything, to criticise me is a bit rich. His only claim to fame is that he beat me twice and, on both occasions, my mum could have beaten me.'

I was happy to have got it off my chest but a letter arrived from snooker's governing body telling me that there was going to be a disciplinary hearing. My attitude was to say 'to hell with them'. I'd made up my mind that I wasn't backing down or apologising. Why should I? They could ban me if they wanted to. My new manager, Pat Mooney, wrote to the governing body insisting that I was only taking the opportunity to reply to McCulloch's remarks. But they were having none of it and insisted that I had to attend a disciplinary hearing. Pat phoned them two days beforehand. 'Graeme is bringing a lawyer with him,' he said. 'Nobody wants this. Everything is just getting out of hand.'

'Just be there,' he was told. 'And bring your lawyer.'

I made it clear to the governing body that I had no intention of apologising. If Ian McCulloch, or any other player, was going to criticise me in any way then I surely had the right to answer them back. 'I was brought up in Easterhouse,' I told them. 'And if that sort of thing had been said there, it would have been dealt with very differently. I thought that I was being diplomatic.'

I was given a warning. I felt vindicated. I would not normally take on the establishment but, on this occasion, I felt like a bit of a rebel and I was quite proud of myself. Ian McCulloch is not on my Christmas-card list and I am not on his. We bump into each other from time to time and we don't speak to each other. I actually live in a pretty close-knit world. You go to tournaments and you see the same faces so it makes sense to make some kind of an effort to get on with them. I am closer to some than to others but I don't have a problem with any of them.

I was feeling shabbily treated at tournaments though. At one match, at a tournament in Ireland in November 2007, I was told that I was playing at 10am, although the television cameras would not be there until 2pm. I am not precious in any way but it is a fact that morning sessions are not especially well-attended and I believed that my success had earned me the right to start my matches either in the afternoon or in the evening. I took it without saying anything but then I was drawn to play Mark Allen, a local lad from Belfast. The next big thing against the world champion – and they put us on an outside table. He beat me and, although I had no problem with the result, I wasn't amused because we both knew that, had we been put on the show table, we would have packed the place to the rafters.

I sought out the tournament director and asked why we had been shunted into the sidings. I was told that RTE, the Irish TV station, had demanded that Ken Doherty be put on the main table, that Mark Allen was from Northern Ireland and, therefore, was not as much of a draw card. It was like a red rag to a bull. 'I don't know how to tell you this,' I said. 'But I am the world champion, not Ken Doherty.'

I continued to be treated that way throughout the 2007/08 season. I played Shaun Murphy on an outside table at the Malta Cup – a game that should obviously have been on TV – and I remember playing my third-round match and realising that Matthew Stevens, who was not having the best of times then, was playing on the TV table. I am delighted to report that it did not affect my form – in a funny way, it may have brought the best out of me.

I have had one or two run-ins with the governing body, which have been laughable. In 2006, after I had won the World Championship, I suggested to the WSA that changing the session times would result in a better quality of final. Their reply told me that I should have kept my thoughts to myself.

It's only natural that a newspaper report will twist the emphasis of what you've told them – they want the best possible story, after all. The governing body, however, takes what it reads as gospel and then issues a warning based on that newspaper article when it would be better to check with the player. And so when I said, 'If they want a better game, surely, if they change the session times, they would get it, but the BBC are in control of that,' the press headline read, DOTT SLAMS BBC. I'm sorry? At no point did I either 'slam' or 'criticise' the BBC – but the truth is that each session of the final starts at a time to suit the BBC.

On another occasion we played in a round-robin tournament, where the early matches were played over the best of five frames. Again, all the players hated it. We were split into groups and there was an obvious flaw with the format, namely that you are bound to end up with a series of dead matches; if somebody lost their first two games, it did not matter whether they won or lost their third because they were already out of the tournament. In one of my matches I needed to win 3-0 to have a chance of going through so, when I lost the first frame, it didn't matter what I did now – I was out of the tournament so all effort was meaningless. Afterwards I said, 'It is a bit weird playing a match where after the first frame I didn't care whether I won or lost. It is hard.' Cue another letter telling me I shouldn't have said that and threatening me with disciplinary action. I used to screw up such letters and throw them straight in the bin.

After Steve Davis beat me at one match at The Crucible, I noted that he went to the toilet at the end of every frame. It was a slow match –excruciatingly so. We only played six frames in the first session when we had been scheduled to play nine. He won all 6 frames but, had he played quicker, he'd have led 9-0. My frustration with the speed of play was reported in a newspaper with DOTT CALLS DAVIS A CHEAT. I had said no such thing. Surprisingly, there was no letter after that.

The only other player I ever had a problem with was Quinten Hann. Australian-born Hann was a flamboyant character who was subsequently thrown out of the game after being found guilty of match fixing. It was a shame because he was a colourful character and on his good days he was the sort of character that snooker needed. Many years ago at Blackpool he beat me 5-0 in a match I didn't enjoy because he started showboating and playing exhibition-style shots, which I thought showed a complete lack of respect. A couple of weeks after that I was drawn to play Hann again and my manager Alex was as psyched up for the match as I was. 'Remember what he did to you the last time you played? Don't give him the sniff of a chance where he can do that again. Just go out there and do to him what he did to you.' I beat him 5-0 and got my own back in some style. There was one frame where I was on an 80-odd break and chose to play safe. I know that it annoyed him but I was loving it. In another frame I got to the last black and doubled it, rather than going for the easy pot. He didn't like it but I felt, if he could dish it out, he should have been able to take it.

Soon after, Hann accused me of bad-mouthing him in the press. 'I haven't the first idea what you are talking about, I really don't,' I told him but he said that he didn't believe me. From that point on there was always an atmosphere when the two of us played – a grudge match if you like. The fact that I generally beat him did not do a great deal for our relationship.

Then we played each other in the Scottish Open. He was not a happy bunny – I quickly built up a 4-0 lead and, after an interval, I required one more frame for victory. I was 66 ahead with 67 on the table and, to his credit, he came to the table and cleared up to reduce my lead to 4-1. This was a great break under pressure because he knew that one mistake could cost him the match.

As he was walking back to his chair he turned to John Williams, the referee, and said, 'I want to change my tip.' Williams asked to see the cue. 'No, there's nothing wrong with it. You can't change it, Quinten,' said Williams. This was the same tip he had just used to make a frame-winning clearance. Hann protested. He was adamant that there was something wrong with his tip – and soon enough it was off.

I was furious and walked over to poor old John Williams. 'I must get the frame here, John,' I said. 'You told him he wasn't allowed to come off.'

'I can't do that, Graeme,' he replied. 'You would need to see the tournament director. I think you should get the frame but that call cannot be my decision.'

I stormed out of the arena and went to find the tournament director, Mike Ganley. In the tournament office, I could see Quinten sitting in a corner putting his new tip on. I gave Mike the full benefit of my opinion.

'What's going on here, Mike? This is a disgrace. How can he possibly get away with doing something like that?'

Mike tried to calm me down, telling me that Quinten had 15 minutes to get his cue ready for play. The Australian was smiling at me. He knew that he had got me angry and I guess that was his intention. I had lost the plot. Alex wandered up to the office to see what was going on. Needless to say, he wasn't happy either. I had to get myself ready to go back out and play again. Hann won the next frame and I began to think that he was going to win the match but I somehow managed to pinch the next one to win the match.

As he came over to shake my hand, I initially put my hand out but then I pulled it away and walked past him. I know that it was a stupid thing to do and I regretted it immediately. In my defence, I couldn't bear to be near him. I shook hands with John Williams and left the arena but Quinten followed me and asked why I had refused to shake his hand. I continued the bad-tempered exchange and, before I knew what was going on, the two of us were shouting at each other. John Williams had to remind us that other matches were being played and that this was no way to behave – and he was right. In the end, Hann went one way and I went the other.

In my defence, he managed to upset a few people. During the Grand Prix in 2001, Anthony Hamilton, who is one of the most mild-mannered individuals you could ever wish to meet, accused Hann of bad sportsmanship. After the World Championships in 2004, Mark King met Hann in a charity boxing match, which Hann actually won.

I attracted some negative press coverage for my clash with Quinten and I regret the incident now – I should have been man enough just to shake his hand and get on with it. We did eventually put our differences behind us and it was Quinten who made the first move, which made him a bigger man than me.

CHAPTER NINETEEN

FIGHTING THE DEMONS

When I finished the 2006–07 season as world No. 2, after John Higgins won the World Championship, and a period of real turbulence in my life, that is when it really hit me. No longer did I have any tournaments to look forward to; no longer was I able to run away and hide from it for a week at a time. There was nothing.

It didn't help that I was upset with the Premier League, the invitation-only event screened on Sky TV. I guess that my invitation must have got lost in the post. In what other sport with a field of seven or eight players would the world's second best player be left out? Yet there was nothing I could do. It was a kick in the balls. The previous year I had been asked because I had been world champion, yet this time I felt my cause was far more deserving as I had performed well over a sustained period. It had been my best ever year.

Maybe some pundits thought I would struggle with the shot

clock, where players only have 25 seconds to play each shot, but I loved that way of playing in 2006: the only player quicker than me was Ronnie O'Sullivan and, when I reached the semi-finals, I was only pipped by Jimmy White (who I had beaten in the league stage). So it's not as if I'd failed to make an impression. I got such a buzz playing there in Glasgow and being introduced as world champion, especially when I could beat Steve Davis in front of my home crowd.

So when you put all that together, you will understand my anger at not receiving an invitation in 2007. The bottom line, however, is that the Premier League organisers can ask whoever they want. And they didn't want me.

I met my new manager Pat Mooney when I was playing in a golf day with John Higgins. Pat asked me how I was getting on without Alex. I told him that I was trying to do things myself and that I was finding some of it quite difficult, especially trying to get interest from sponsors.

'I think I could maybe help you with that,' he said. 'I've got contacts and I don't mind approaching people on your behalf.' I agreed that he could see what he could do for me. Once again, there was no contract, just a shake of the hands. If he could find me a sponsor I would be happy to give him a cut. There was no way that my table earnings were up for grabs – I was taking care of paying my entry fees and getting myself to and from tournaments.

Pat found me a sponsor and started working with John too. Before we knew where we were, he was talking about his dream for a world series of snooker, a world tour independent of the World Snooker Association. Pat wanted to see the tour grow to such an extent that it would eventually come under the umbrella of the WSA. The next thing I heard was that he had launched it with John as his star attraction. It could have bothered me but it really didn't. In the end they were little more than exhibitions. We went to Poland, where John, Mark Selby, Steve Davis and I played but Pat wanted more and it grew to eight players. There were four tournaments, with a grand final, and it was fine. Pat was looking after John and I, and it meant that, when people phoned, I could put them in touch with Pat and leave him to take care of my schedule. That relationship was to end in tears too.

The summer of 2007 was the most difficult of my life. I'd had depression for many, many months. There were days when I could barely function and I vividly recall fantasising about the different ways that it would be possible to end my life. I never seriously thought about pushing ahead with any of them but something was seriously wrong.

At least Elaine was on the road to recovery and was attending college as she completed her training to become a nurse. She has always been the practical one in our relationship and decided that she wanted to learn a skill that would allow her to earn money in case the day ever came when I couldn't earn enough. She used to take Lewis to a nursery at the college and I was left alone at home to brood. She would go out at 8am and come back almost eight hours later. One day she went out and I was sitting on the sofa in the lounge and, when she got home, I hadn't moved. There was no television on. I had been sitting like a zombie all day long, just staring into space.

As the 2007–08 season approached, I wasn't prepared for it. My usual practice routine involved getting in the car and driving into Glasgow to a club where I played with John Higgins, but I couldn't really face it and, even on the days when I was there, I might as well have stayed at home. I would be walking into the club and the tears would be rolling down my cheeks but I would compose myself. I would get back in the car and cry all the way home – again, I would take a deep breath and get my act together before walking into the house. The best therapy would have been to have a good cry with Elaine and to tell her about my feelings but I was unable to do that.

There was no respite when the snooker season got under way because I would head off to a tournament and lose in the first round, come home, head off to the next event and lose in the first round. I felt nothing and the worst thing of all was I didn't care.

My ranking started to plummet and I lost something like 14 matches on the trot. The press, of course, did not take long to pick up on my slump but they hadn't a clue what was causing it and I didn't realise what was going on inside my head. At the Wales Open, when I played Michael Judge, things were so bad that I missed the pack of reds with my break-off shot. It was something I had never done even as a child. I laughed it off, Michael laughed and the referee laughed but that match was due to start at 4pm and I didn't get out of bed until about an hour or so before it began. Nor did I have anything to eat before I played. As I waited that day at the hotel for the car to take me to the arena in Newport, I saw John Higgins walking in. He was and is one of my best friends in snooker but I hid behind a pillar so that he wouldn't see me.

After that defeat by Judge I felt hopeless. I wasn't making any money so I couldn't see any point in it. I was going to a lot of tournaments on my own and that didn't help because it meant I was alone with my thoughts. I used to look at the passenger seat and cry because Alex wasn't there. I didn't win a game all year but I remained in the top 16 at the end of the 2007–08 season because I had started it with so many ranking points. Provisionally, I was ranked number 40, which meant that I had to start winning matches or I would be back to playing qualifiers, which were now staged in Prestatyn instead of Blackpool.

In short, I had stopped enjoying my snooker. It gave me no pleasure at all to pot a long red or to win a frame. If I wasn't motivated to get up in the morning, I sure as hell wasn't motivated to chase a white ball around a table covered in green baize. It all seemed so pointless to me. I was going to tournaments without having practised and I wouldn't pick up my cue while I was there until I had to play my match. Even so, and I know it doesn't make any sense, it still hurt to lose.

Before long, I couldn't concentrate on anything. I would be out in the car with Elaine and she would say, 'Graeme, you're going the wrong way.' If I couldn't focus on a journey to the shops, how would I be able to concentrate on a frame of snooker, where you have to think not only of the shot you are playing but also of the ones you will be playing in two, three or four shots time? It was all that I could do to hit the cue ball.

Several times during that ill-fated season I also hit the wrong ball. Convinced that I could get to a particular red, I would go for it and miss it by a mile because the shot was never on. That sort of thing played havoc with my mind because I would come back to the table for the next frame and I would start to question the things I was seeing.

If a Rangers game was showing on television, I couldn't care less whether they won, lost or drew. Normally if Rangers scored a goal I would be jumping up and down. Even if my friend Jim would phone, I would get Elaine to tell him I was in the bath.

Even straightforward routine tasks seemed beyond me. I have always taken it upon myself to lock up the house last thing at night. I would go into the kitchen, lock the back door, switch off the lights, lock the front door and check that the television was switched off. One morning Elaine came back upstairs to tell me that I had left all the lights on and the back door wide open. I was living my life in a daze.

It was after the Wales Open defeat at the hands of Michael Judge that a small light came on in my head. I told Elaine that I hadn't felt right for months and that I had to tell somebody. Straight away she said, 'Maybe you've got depression.' I wouldn't hear of it. I didn't fully understand what depression was but I was sure that I didn't have it. When I spoke to my mum, she suggested I should have a word with Dad and said that he had also suffered quite badly with depression. It helped me to know that he had come out the other side. And then I discovered that Uncle George had been through it too and, in fact, still suffers with it.

Through it all, I had put a terrible strain on my marriage. It all came to a head one day when Elaine and I were on a day out. In a car park she told me that she had just about reached the end of her tether with me; that I needed to get myself sorted out. It was all too much for me. All the emotion that I had suppressed suddenly came to the surface and, when I started crying, I didn't think that I would ever stop but I poured out my heart and soul out. Elaine believed I was almost suicidal but this was the wake-up call I needed.

I went to see my doctor and was given a list of things to go through, like a checklist for depression. As I was going through the list, I felt a sense of relief because I realised that this was what was wrong with me but I still broke down in tears as I was going through the list. It seemed that I suffered from every symptom. At the end of it the doctor confirmed that I was, indeed, suffering from depression.

In March 2008 I was given a course of anti-depressants. About two weeks later I had to play Barry Pinches in the China Open. Whenever I got anywhere near a snooker table, even at that point, I went to pieces. During the game I started crying. I couldn't believe what was happening to me. Fortunately, there wasn't too big a crowd in the arena.

Barry was 3-1 ahead and was in the middle of a clearance that would put him 4-1 in front. I had gone from achieving almost all of my dreams to a point where absolutely anybody was beating me – and I mean no disrespect to Barry when I say that. As the thoughts went through my mind, the tears started to roll down my cheeks. Nobody in the crowd saw it but I couldn't help myself and I couldn't stop, so I grabbed my towel and put it over my face. Finally I managed to stop crying and held myself together long enough to lose 5-1 but my eyes were red raw from the tears.

Afterwards I got back to the hotel, got changed and went for something to eat with John Higgins. During that meal I told him that I wasn't going to play in the 2008 World Championships. 'I can't control my emotions. If I am crying in China, I don't want to put myself in a position where the same thing happens at The Crucible in front of millions of television viewers,' I told him. 'When you add the pressure of that tournament, I just don't feel that I am in a position to be able to cope with it at present. The media would have a field day.'

John was shocked. We were joined by Stephen Maguire and I also told him but, even as I was speaking to them, I could feel the tears welling up. I announced that my plan was to take a year out, but then I had to change the subject.

On a ten-hour flight home from China I also confided in another player, Fergal O'Brien, telling him about my plan to take a sabbatical. He suggested I attended the World Championship and to just wait and see. 'After that the season will be over,' he reasoned, 'and you will have a few months to see how you feel. You might find that you've got your head right. If, at the end of that time, you still feel the same way, it might be the right thing to take a year out. But I reckon you're jumping the gun.'

Fergal's words sounded sensible but I worried I would not be able to cope so I maintained that I was withdrawing from the tournament. I repeated my vow to my manager Pat Mooney, my parents, brother and my friend Jim – I wasn't ready to take part in the World Championship. I'm sure everyone was relieved that I was taking a break, although Pat was concerned that I was being too hasty. 'Listen, Graeme, if you want me to put out a press release, I will do it,' he said. 'But I am going to hold on to it for a couple of days because by then you might feel differently.'

'I appreciate what you are trying to do, Pat,' I replied, 'but I haven't just woken up this morning and come to this decision. It's something I have been thinking about for quite some time and I know it is the right thing to do. I can't put myself through it. My health has to come first.'

Two days later I told him to go ahead and issue the press release. Now that I had made up my mind, I felt a huge weight lifting from my shoulders. Strangely, I felt good.

But Pat had a suggestion. 'Listen, I have been speaking to a friend of mine. He's a psychologist and I believe it might help you to have a chat with him. Would you mind doing that before we do anything else?' His name was Bob Burns and he was based in Perth. He was a genuinely nice man and I was able to relate to him almost straight away.

'I am not here to put any pressure on you, Graeme,' Bob said. 'But I'm convinced that I can help you sufficiently for you to be able to go and play at The Crucible. The reason you are at your worst and have been having the crying episodes while playing snooker is because the game and everything about it reminds you of Alex. That's the part of your brain we need to get sorted out and we can do it.'

It all went straight over my head to begin with but, the more I listened to him, the more what he was saying seemed to make sense. 'You can be sitting playing cards or whatever and everything is fine,' he said. 'But as soon as you have to get yourself ready for a snooker match you don't want to play. I would also like to bet that you are not really practising either. Your brain can't handle the pain of what you have been through with Alex. It doesn't want to deal with it so it just shuts off. You will not have any concentration or focus but I can get you to the point where you will, at least, be able to play.'

Everything Bob had said to me was uncannily accurate and I told Pat not to release the press statement. In my heart of hearts I wanted to go to Sheffield because I knew that the press would have a field day at my expense if I didn't. I did not want to be remembered as the former world champion who didn't go to The Crucible when he was qualified to do so.

Bob did some hypnosis work and taught me various relaxation techniques, focusing on getting his message across to my unconscious brain. He gave me a series of mental keys but, most importantly, I knew that I was with someone who understood what I was going through because he had seen it before in other people. And it also helped to know that I wasn't a freak and that I wasn't a one-off. Other people suffered in precisely the same way. It is difficult to put into words the sense of relief I felt to know that I wasn't losing my marbles and that this was a man who could help to snap me out of it. Every time I would tell him something, he would tell me why I was feeling that way. I hadn't realised but, subconsciously, I had been grieving for Alex every time I played snooker.

We had three or four sessions where Bob encouraged me to talk about Alex and to discuss how I was feeling, and it began to help. On top of that, I had now been on the anti-depressants for a while and Bob helped me progress to a point where I could actually go to the World Championship. Rather than blotting Alex out, Bob wanted to encourage me to imagine I had him there with me, looking after me. I began to feel much brighter but my biggest concern was that I hadn't prepared for the tournament. I didn't want to go to Sheffield and make a complete and utter fool of myself. I had been worrying that I would start crying but now I was concerned that I would not be able to pot a ball.

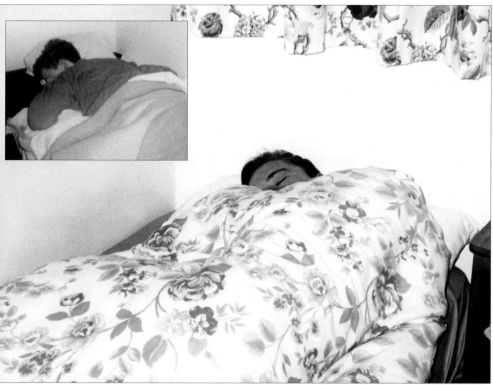

Above: Mum's the word. Elaine and I with my Mum, who has been through her own health battles.

Bottom: Dreaming of glory. I admit that bed has always been one of my favourite places.

Above: Family man – with Elaine and my wonderful children, Lewis and Lucy, the reason I get up in the morning.

Left: Cheers! Alex raises a glass to my future.

Right: Birthday boy – cutting into a cake made to look like a snooker table.

Above: Collecting a trophy after winning a junior tournament – don't I look all grown up?

Below left: A Pontin's holiday camp not looking like the most glamorous place in the world

Below right: Alexander and I enjoy a day out with Lewis.

Getting ready to make
another century break.

Left: Silver service – I may have had to wait a while to win a tournament as a professional, but I had no such worries as a junior.

Right: Beating the big boys – receiving my trophy for winning the under-19 tournament at Pontin's when I was just 15.

...hrough the years… Boy wonder (*above*). At home with my parents – you will notice ...at the cue is bigger than I am and (*below*) with some of my fellow professionals after ...inning the 2006 World Championship. Back row, from left, Willie Thorne, John Parrott, ...ephen Hendry and Ian McCulloch. Front row, from left, Stephen Maguire, yours truly, ...mie Burnett, Dennis Taylor and Matthew Stevens.

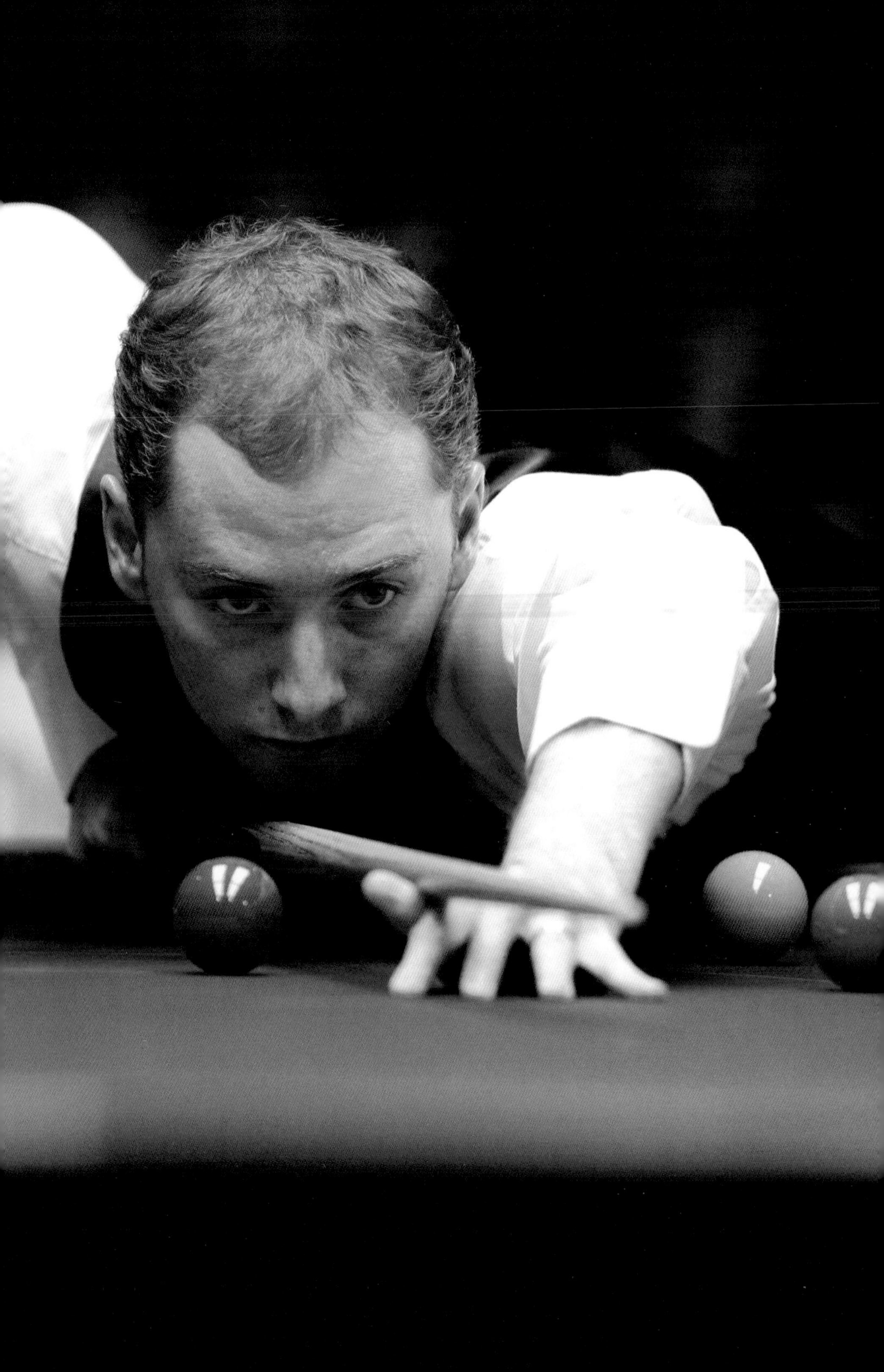

Playing in the UK championships in 2006.
© Rex Features

I was relieved that we hadn't issued the press statement because there would have been nothing worse than to have told the public I wasn't going to compete and then do a U-turn. Cynics could have suggested I had announced my withdrawal in order to get public sympathy, while always intending to play. I had already been in touch with the governing body and made some enquiries about taking a year out of the sport. I wanted to know what the implications were, whether my ranking could be protected and that kind of thing, so I was deadly serious about it all.

But if I hadn't been able to prepare properly, my achievement in 2008 was just to be at The Crucible and get through it all in one piece. I set myself the target of playing half-decent snooker, nothing more than that. I faced Joe Perry and, although he beat me 10-7, I took a great deal of satisfaction from that performance. It was the first time in as long as I could remember that I had played well and enjoyed it. Joe had four centuries so I lost to a man at the peak of his game. I don't like losing but there was no shame in my game.

The press somehow got wind of the fact that I had been considering withdrawing from the tournament and, when I got to Sheffield, I was aware of some whispers. I knew that the only way to deal with it was to speak to them about what had been going on. It also helped them to understand the dreadful run of form I had endured and I was quite relieved to get the thing out in the open. And the upshot was that, after it had appeared in the newspapers, when I walked into the arena to play Joe I received a warm welcome from the crowd. It meant a great deal to realise that people who didn't know me could care so much about what I had been going through. It was another little piece of the jigsaw falling back into place on my road to recovery. The Crucible crowd like previous winners and I have always had a good rapport with them but that was particularly special. I remember telling myself not to cry, although at least that would have been for the right reason.

That World Championship tournament at The Crucible was the turning point for me. I could now see some light, even though I would begin the 2008–09 season ranked 13th in the world and with virtually no chance of remaining in the top 16. In the event, I fell to 28th for 2009–10 and was lucky not to tumble out of the top 32.

I felt that my own personal hell was now over and, to a large extent, it was. For the record, the worst of my results during that awful period were as follows:

October 2007: Grand Prix, group games, lost to Ali Carter 4-3, lost to Marcus Campbell 4-2, lost to Anthony Hamilton 4-0, lost to Michael Holt 4-1.

November 2007: Northern Ireland Trophy, second round (first round, bye), lost to Mark Allen 5-3.

December 2007: UK Championship, first round, lost to Dave Harold 9-7.

January 2008: Saga Insurance Masters, first round, lost to Stephen Lee 6-5.

February 2008: Malta Cup, group games, lost to Dominic Dale 4-2, drew with Ding Junhui 3-3, lost to Mark Williams 4-2, lost to Peter Ebdon 4-2.

February 2008: Wales Open, second round (first round, bye), lost to Michael Judge 5-4.

March 2008: China Open, first round, lost to Barry Pinches 5-1.

My problems as I entered the 2008–09 season were that I was desperately short on confidence and everybody else on the circuit felt they would beat me with their eyes closed. I hadn't officially taken a year off but my form had been so bad the previous season that I may as well have done. For the new season I still had to go away and practise as hard as I possibly could but now it became easier because I no longer dreaded picking up a cue.

The 2008–09 season began with another defeat for me – in August in Northern Ireland I lost 5-3 to Dave Harold, even though I had played all right – but then in September it was off to China for the Shanghai Masters. Some of the boys announced that they were going to play football. Did I fancy joining them? I did not need to be asked twice. We were playing a four-a-side match. There was me, Mark Williams, Ryan Day, Tom Ford, Brandon Parker (Shaun Murphy's manager) and Mark Selby's manager. Mark was watching from the sidelines.

After Tom hit a shot I instinctively put my left hand out to stop it and flicked it past the post. As I ran to get the ball I was suddenly aware of a really sharp shooting pain. I didn't want to yelp like a wee girl but it was bloody painful. I thought that I had sprained it so I just played on but the pain increased and I walked over to Mark Selby because he had some water. As I reached for the drink I looked down at my wrist and it was swollen and disfigured. I knew that I had broken it, a suspicion that was confirmed by Brandon. And so I was forced to withdraw from both the Shanghai Masters and the Grand Prix, scheduled to take place back in Glasgow in October.

My wrist was pretty badly broken, with a couple of broken

bones and a fracture, and I had to wear a heavy-duty cast on my bridge hand. I did try to see if I could play but it was impossible. Any hope I may have had of remaining in the top 16 was now rapidly fading and I was going stir crazy. The next tournament was the Bahrain Championship in November and, had I kept the cast on for as long as the doctors wanted, I'd have had to miss that as well.

When I asked the doctors if the cast could be removed a few days early so that I could play in Bahrain they agreed – but only on condition that I agreed to absolve them of all responsibility if it did not heal properly. I was happy to go along with that and the very next day I was on the plane to Bahrain. With no snooker practice for six weeks, the chances of achieving anything were slim but I at least wanted to give myself the chance. It was a strain: Barry Pinches beat me 5-3 in the first round. I was able to form a bridge with my left hand but I couldn't pick up the rest with it and it hurt whenever I had to stretch to play shots.

Early in 2008 Elaine and I had felt broody, and we agreed that it would be great to give Lewis a brother or a sister. In no time at all Elaine fell pregnant again and, on 27 November 2008, Lucy was born. Now I had a further incentive to find my game again. We had always agreed that we only wanted two children so I immediately went away and had the snip.

It wasn't until the UK Championship in December that I finally stopped the rot in my game, beating Ken Doherty 9-4. It tasted sweet. No matter how good you are, you start to wonder if you will ever win a match again. Finally my losing run was over and the press were off my back. Thank goodness. I lost to Mark Williams 9-7 in a hard-fought second-round match but, by now, I believed that I might be able to climb back up the rankings.

The New Year even found me putting up a decent showing against Stephen Maguire in the first round of The Masters, although he eventually came out on top 6-5. Next I won another first-round game at the Wales Open, beating Mike Dunn 5-3 before succumbing to Ali Carter. But it was at the China Open at the end of March 2009 where my fortunes really started to take a turn for the better.

In the first round in Beijing I faced Yu Delu, a Chinese player who had beaten Rod Lawler in the wild-card round. Naturally, he had all the local support. Twelve months earlier I would have collapsed like a pack of cards but this time I held my nerve under the most severe pressure to beat him 5-3. Through to the second round, I thrashed Mark Selby 5-1 in a match that really meant something to me because it proved that I could once again compete against and beat the best players in the world. My good form only faltered in the quarter-finals, where I lost to England's Stuart Pettman but, overall, I took a lot of positives from that tournament.

Back at The Crucible in Sheffield for the World Championship I beat Barry Hawkins in the first round. On the face of it, this was just another game but, for me, it was almost as big as playing in the final. Had Barry won, I would have dropped out of the top 32, never mind top 16, but to my enormous relief, I managed to win 10-8. I could just about live with being the world's 28th ranked player because I knew it was going to be a temporary state of affairs. Then the second round promised a rematch with Mark Selby, obviously still smarting from the defeat I inflicted upon him in China because he beat me 13-10.

I had been up there with the very best and I wanted it again. How could a player be in the top 16, drop out and still think that things were going all right? They were crumbs of comfort after the depths I had plumbed. If my ranking had fallen beyond 32, I'd have been back to the days of needing to win 2 qualifying matches to reach the knockout stages of every tournament.

Meanwhile, the anti-depressants were helping. I had become aware of an occasional day when I felt normal again and, as the days turned into weeks, I was able to identify all sorts of positives. I could not only sit down and talk with Elaine but I actually looked forward to coming home and having catch-up conversations. I wasn't getting lost on the road anymore. I would offer to help Elaine in the kitchen. My sleep patterns returned to some kind of normality. I would no longer sit around the house for hours on end. My appetite started to return and I even got a little bit of colour in my cheeks. I no longer felt that I was going to burst into tears. I even found that, if I had been watching TV, I could actually remember what it was that I'd seen. Elaine even told me that she was pleased to see me playing the occasional game of online poker again, even if it did mean that I lost a little bit of money.

Best of all, I had begun to regain my motivation – I wanted to do things and I wanted to play snooker. In November 2008, just before Lucy was born, I decided to have a snooker room built on the side of the house so that I could start working hard on my game. I could think of Alex and remember the good times, and I could smile at the recollections, rather than feel nothing but despair, as I had in the days before the pills and sessions with Bob Burns. The purpose began to return to my life.

I had been warned, however, that I might need to take anti-depressants for the rest of my life. There may be times when I could go months without them but there was always a chance that something might trigger the depression again. The great thing was that I would know what to do if it happened again. Initially, I might have three days a week where I felt good. I was on them for about three months and, although I didn't feel great, I woke up one day and thought, Right, I can manage now. This is the way I am meant to feel.

I began to come to terms with the fact that depression was something I was going to have to learn to live with. I was on the tablets for the thick end of a year and then went back to see the doctor because I felt well enough to try and cope without them. The doctor agreed that I should wean myself off them gradually and I was fine for a long time after that, although I have since been back on them after realising that I was starting to slip. I didn't need anybody to tell me. I know the difference now between the natural lows that everybody feels from time and that darkness that is a part of depression, so I am now able to ask for help without being ashamed or embarrassed.

It's a funny thing but, since I suffered from depression, I have become far more aware of my emotions. I don't want any of you to think that I have become an emotional cripple because that certainly isn't the case; maybe it is just that I appreciate things more now. I no longer take anything for granted.

I had finally got over the death of Alex. I was asked whether I felt he was looking over me when I was a finalist at Sheffield in 2010. He might well have been but I didn't feel that way. I would rather not talk about him and about what happened to him but at least I was now able to deal with it without finding myself retreating into a dark place. Some people cope by talking about loss but I would still rather keep my thoughts to myself. I will always have feelings for him, however briefly, when I win important matches because, without him, I may never have got to the place I am now.

CHAPTER TWENTY
THE LONG ROAD BACK 2009/10

*I*n the summer of 2009 I had to head off to the qualifiers at Prestatyn, a place I remembered well from my days as an up-and-coming amateur. Never in my worst nightmares had I imagined that I would ever be required to come back here but at least I only had to win one match for each tournament to reach the business end. At the Blackpool qualifiers years before I had pitied the likes of Tony Knowles and Mike Hallett, vowing that nobody would ever find me in such a situation – trying to scratch a living but being beaten time and time again by the stars of tomorrow. And it made a huge difference to me that I now had a family back at home. Being away from them while I was earning decent money playing in a ranking tournament was one thing but being stuck in Prestatyn on my own was something else entirely. I hated it and everything it stood for. The likes of promising stars like Judd Trump reminded me of how I had been.

At Prestatyn I was playing in front of six people when I had been used to playing at The Crucible and on television. The depression was under control by now but I had fallen out of love with the game. When I was playing well I would happily practise for hours but now it was as much as I could do to concentrate for an hour. There had been signs of playing well at The Crucible but I had to do it all year round, in every tournament. It did briefly enter my head that, perhaps, my career was finished but I knew that I didn't want to end it in Prestatyn.

I asked Hunt and Osborne, a cue-maker based in London, to make me a new cue. They sent me five. I had made up my mind that I wanted a maple cue and they sent me one but, although I loved the way it felt, I was playing incredibly badly with it. If I tried to screw the ball back two inches, I was instead stunning the cue ball. It never once entered my head that it could be anything to do with the cue. I had no feel with the cue but decided to use it in a match-conditions competition so I took it with me to play Marcus Campbell and he beat me 5-1. I decided to discard the maple cue and picked up one made from ash.

The difference was immediate. I got my sense of feel back but there was only a week left before my first qualifying match. I made up my mind that I would stick with the ash cue and my friend Jim came with me on the long drive to North Wales. Jim had been with me through thick and thin, both at the World Championship and now at Prestatyn. I was playing a youngster called Jimmy Robertson and watching were Jim and two other people. If you ever want to be reminded of how quickly a sportsman can fall, this is the place to visit.

Before I knew where I was, Robertson was 3-1 ahead. He had come through from the very first round of qualifying so he was match ready and I was not. I didn't move at the interval, electing to remain in my chair and rage quietly at how badly I was playing. This had nothing to do with depression. I found myself looking around the place and thinking, What the hell am I doing here? I never felt that I was too good to be there – my results proved that I deserved to be. I felt I was only there because I'd had 12 months of depression.

As Robertson won a further frame after the interval, stretching his lead to 4-1, I felt so angry with myself that I decided to throw caution to the wind. I went for absolutely everything and flew around the table like Ronnie O'Sullivan on speed. And do you know what? The balls were disappearing into the pockets and, before I knew where I was, I had won 5-4.

I was driving home with Jim, having just qualified to play in China, and I said to him, 'You know what, mate? I could chuck it. I could give this up, dead easy.'

'What on earth are you talking about?' he replied.

'I have won a match and I should be happy but I'm not. It's not that I am depressed again or anything like that, it's just that I didn't get any enjoyment from it.'

If somebody had given me something else to do at that point, I would have grabbed it with both hands. Jim found it difficult to understand so I tried to elaborate.

'I am calm here. I have just won a match that I should, perhaps, have lost so I should be buzzing – but I am not,' I told him. 'If you offered me the opportunity to be your partner in a business venture right now and you could guarantee me

£30,000 a year, I would do it. I would walk away from snooker in a heartbeat.'

My next visit to China certainly didn't restore my love of the game. Ronnie O'Sullivan thrashed me 5-0. On my return I decided to discard the ash cue and try one of the others that Hunt and Osborne had sent me. I didn't like that either. Two days before I was due to go back to Prestatyn for another qualifier, I picked up another cue, played fellow Scot Jamie Burnett and he beat me 5-0.

Now I was saying to Jim, 'I have left school with no qualifications – what else can I do? There must be something. I have always thought the Scottish Parliament should fund a snooker academy and, if I can persuade them to set one up, I will be prepared to work for them as a coach if they give me a living wage.'

'But you are far too good to be doing that.'

'Didn't you just watch that match against Jamie? Didn't you just see me losing five-zero?'

It actually wasn't as bad a defeat as it looks on paper. I lost three frames on the black, one on the pink and the other on a re-spotted black, so I could just as easily have won 5-0 but there was no way I could see it. In the end, I don't think Jim knew what to say next or what to expect. He told me I would get through it but I didn't know if I wanted to.

Before my non-appearance at the Masters, December 2009 had found me at the UK Championship but, when I faced Mark Williams, he had a walkover when illness forced me to pull out of the tournament. It was as if I'd caught a dose of the flu. I tried Vitamin C and paracetamol, and might have tried something else, but that would have risked failing a drugs test.

We have a list of banned substances and you wouldn't believe how long it is.

Trailing Mark Williams by 6-2 at the end of the first session, I felt dizzy and had a thumping headache. All I wanted to do was sleep so I phoned the tournament director, Mike Ganley, from my hotel, withdrew from the match and fell asleep straight away. Even driving back to Glasgow, I felt so poorly that I had to stop every 40 minutes or so because I kept feeling that I was going to fall asleep at the wheel of the car. Back at home a couple of days later, I was giving my daughter Lucy her breakfast when I felt particularly nauseous. Looking in the mirror, I was white as a sheet and the sweat was pouring from my body so I stripped off all my clothes and lay on the cold tiles on the bathroom floor. Elaine opened the window and I am sure she believed I was in the process of having a heart attack. She asked me if I had chest pains. I didn't but it turned out my blood pressure had plummeted. Yet, mysteriously, the frightening feeling soon passed and has never returned.

At the same time, Barry Hearn – who had become Chairman of the World Snooker Association – was starting to talk about dragging the game out of the dark ages but did I want to be part of that or not? The players were coming into the venue to music and there seemed to be a new enthusiasm and atmosphere which had been missing under the chairmanship of Hearn's predecessor, Rodney Walker.

Under Walker's tenure as chairman, the schedule ran to a pretty paltry six tournaments. Walker was not an approachable man but he was a good businessman and, on his departure, the WSA had £3m in the bank. It was there for a

207

rainy day, apparently. Call me old-fashioned if you like but I would have thought that, when you have a schedule that runs to a paltry six tournaments, it must be raining pretty heavily. There were also events where the winner was playing for £30,000. I know that it is still a lot but think about the players who were knocked out in the first round – they were being paid next to nothing.

I remember a telephone conversation with a WSA board member. They were trying to stage the Malta Cup and the prize money on offer was pathetic. When I asked why we needed to travel all the way to Malta for such little reward, he replied, 'Graeme, would you rather we didn't have the tournament?'

'Yes,' I replied.

'What do you mean? That's not a good attitude.'

'If you run this tournament for such small prize money, how on earth can you expect to run another event for, say, twice the prize money? The point is that the second tournament would know they could get it on the cheap, so why would they want to pay out more?'

'Well, Graeme, it is either this or we have fewer tournaments.'

'To be honest, I believe most of the players would rather we have fewer tournaments than be asked to play for what amounts to next to nothing. How can you go to a sponsor and ask him to give you £100,000 to the winner when he knows you have put on an entire event where the total prize money was half that?'

I feel strongly about this, not because the players should be greedy but because we deserve the opportunity to make a living. We should be seeing huge tournaments in China, a country which can afford to stage them and which has a vast television audience. Even if they made it pay-per-view coverage in China, they would still make a fortune.

If you follow snooker you will know that players are expected to dress smartly, wearing a waistcoat and a bowtie. I am in favour of maintaining such standards. It would be difficult to change things without players beginning to look scruffy. We did experiment at a tournament a few years ago, where one player would wear a collared blue T-shirt while his opponent wore a red one, rather like in the game of bowls. The players were not too keen because none of us could see the point.

Barry Hearn has some great ideas for bringing snooker's image into the 21st century. He is prepared to try things until he finds the right formula. If you look at what he has achieved with darts, we should be pretty excited to have him on our side. It's possible to have a proper grown-up phone conversation with him, which was never the case with his predecessors.

The turning point in my recent career finally came in January 2010, when I was in my snooker room practising. The Masters was on television and, for the first time in a number of years, it was taking place without me. As I watched the coverage, I was reflecting on Barry's visions for the future of the game. I was struck at how Rob Walker, introducing the players at Wembley, was working the crowd into a frenzy. Each player had picked their favourite piece of music to enter the arena, to be accompanied by the stamping, cheering crowd. I could also see the hunger in Mark Selby's eyes as he played – a hunger that I used to have. If there was a best-of-three in Bahrain for a prize of £20, Mark would go and take part because he loves the thrill of competing.

And suddenly, I knew that I didn't really want to become a coach at my imaginary Scottish academy after all. The light had gone back on in my head and I wanted to be part of the game again. My passion had returned in a flash and I couldn't wait to get started every day. I told Elaine that she wouldn't see me for four or five hours because I was going to practise. Then I would be on the phone to fellow professionals, such as Marcus Campbell, asking him if wanted to come over for a game.

I did not want to be remembered as the guy who won the world title in 2006 and then just as quickly disappeared. I had some tough draws in the qualifiers, including twice having to play Ken Doherty. Two months earlier he would have beaten me easily but now I was back. I didn't want him to pot a single ball – I became greedy. I was happy to play a tactical game and stop him from potting a ball. I would pot a long red and stun for the black. The shot would come off exactly as I had imagined it would and I was getting a buzz again. I couldn't wait to get to the table. When I beat Doherty, I knew that I could beat anybody in the game. This is what I was born to do.

Even the issues with my cue were resolved. After Jamie Burnett had thrashed me in a qualifier, I had changed it yet again. This replacement cue was ideal and I'm still using it. There may have been nothing wrong with the others, just that my mental attitude hadn't been right. All the grit and determination was back and I was ready to take on anyone.

My first opportunity to show my new-found energy came at

the Wales Open. I eased past the seeded Joe Perry in the opening round by 5-3 but then came up against John Higgins firing on all cylinders and he beat me 5-1. Similar disappointment came at the China Open in Beijing, where I suffered a 5-2 first-round defeat at the hands of Mark Allen. On paper, my record for that season looked unimpressive but my form hadn't been that bad and I didn't count the UK tournaments for that season because I hadn't been well.

Additionally, I had drawn Jimmy Michie in a qualifier for the World Championship, a game I felt I had to win. The pressures felt at a qualifier are entirely different from those you experience at a tournament proper. What made matters worse was that the table wasn't running properly. I would hit the cue ball over the spots and watch as it rolled back down the table. It was miles off centre. The referee agreed to fetch the table fitters during the interval but they told us they couldn't find anything wrong.

'You've got to be having a laugh,' I said. 'It's a disgrace, and Jimmy and I both think so.' Mike Ganley suggested that we go out and demonstrate what was happening, and we duly did. We started by rolling the cue ball down the table and, by the time it got to the other end, it had veered off by two or three inches. It was unplayable. After a lengthy wait, the fitters told us that they couldn't do anything about the table because they were sure the slate was warped. There was no other free table so we had to wait for a game on another table to finish before we could continue. Finally, we were allotted a perfect table and I was raring to get back. I had not started well against Jimmy but now I managed to defeat him and I had qualified once more for the World Championship.

Before we went to the tournament I played lots of practice frames against John Higgins and it proved to be perfect preparation. He doesn't miss balls so the only way that you can beat him is by doing the same thing and it tends to focus the mind. I was making lots of big breaks. It is like playing against a robot so, if you can get near him, it means you are playing well.

One day he was 4-1 ahead and I decided to go for any ball I could see. I had been playing many great safety shots against him and then he would roll in a red and clear up, so I figured it was time to fight fire with fire and it worked. John turned round to me after one particularly outrageous pot and asked, 'Would you have gone for that in a game?' John eventually beat me 10-8 but I felt that I was on to something that I could turn to in a proper match situation.

It worked so well that I took the thought process to Sheffield with me. I made up my mind before I got there that nobody was going to tie me up in knots; that I was going to play quickly and freely and see what happened.

We had rented a flat in Sheffield for the duration of the 2010 tournament. With Dad, Jim and I sharing, it was like a boys' holiday. Every morning Jim would cook breakfast and we would always have French toast – whatever else it may have been, healthy it was not. Dad took control of dinner each night. It is probably worth pointing out that my dad can't cook but he would never admit that. Each night he would produce a burnt offering and each night he would blame the cooker. It was all great fun.

My World Championship journey kicked off with a match against Peter Ebdon. I wasn't in the top 16 so I knew that I was going to be facing a quality player in the first round. Luckily for me, Peter had been struggling throughout the season so he was probably the ideal opponent. He was under enormous pressure in order to keep his place in the 16, whereas I was the underdog, the role I love. I knew that, if I had a decent run, I was likely to get some good press for once. The media likes the sportsman or woman who has been through the mill and has fought back, although no journalist quite knew how close I had come to jacking it all in.

It was important for me to be on the attack as much as possible against Ebdon, rather than the duel turning into a dour safety battle. I led him 7-2 after the first session, knowing I had played very well, but Peter caught me up in the second session. I won 10-5 but I felt that I had stumbled over the line to win and wanted to finish as triumphantly as I had begun.

On the other hand, I had knocked out the 14th seed and was through to the second round, where I would meet Stephen Maguire, ranked 3rd in the world. I know Stephen well – a fellow Scot, he is a naturally gifted player capable of brilliant bursts of scoring. It is hard to play a friend but, when we got out there, he wanted to batter my brains in and I wanted to do the same to him. Stephen didn't start well at all and I took that first session 7-1 – a dream start for me.

Sometimes, like Ronnie O'Sullivan, Stephen can seem to lose interest if things are not going his way and I began to sense that he wasn't happy. But I couldn't be complacent: I needed to win another six frames to get me over the finishing line. And what sort of press would I have received had my opponent presented me with a stunning fight-back?

So that second session was crucial and a series of big breaks propelled me to an 11-1 lead. I only needed two more frames to win, while he had to win all four remaining frames of the session. He clawed 3 frames back so it was now 11-4 in my favour and we gained one frame each, meaning that I narrowly failed to clinch the match with a session to spare.

Because Stephen is a friend, I wouldn't have wanted to beat him by that sort of margin and I am pleased that we had to come back for a third and final session. He rattled off a couple of frames to reduce the deficit to 12-6 but he was never going to get back into it and I won 13-6.

I had already decided that I wasn't practising during the Championship, as I didn't want to use up all my energy on a practice table. I was also having so much fun with Dad and Jim at the flat that I wanted to spend as much time with them as possible. We shared quality time, playing cards and watching the horse racing on television.

My opponent in the quarter-finals was Mark Allen from Northern Ireland, a superb potter, and in this game I intended to go for broke because I felt it presented me with my best opportunity to win. I don't know where my cockiness had come from. Perhaps I felt that snooker owed me something after everything I had been through.

I tried to explain my self-belief to Jim. 'I did it with John in practice and it worked,' I said. 'I reckon that, if I turn this into a potting competition, I can beat him. If I play good safety, he is such a glorious potter that he is going to keep going for long reds. Eventually he will put one away and he will win the frame anyway, so I might as well play him at his own game.'

As always with me, though, nothing is ever

straightforward. On the morning of the game against Allen I woke up with a sore throat and, by the time I got into the arena, I also had chronic earache, which I have never had before or since. Worse still, Mark reeled off the first four frames of the match. Bunged up and struggling to breathe, and with no sign of the earache abating, I began to consider that I might have to withdraw from a match for the second time this season. I eventually managed to get a little bit of relief by making my ears pop, before pulling back three frames. This should have levelled the game but Mark moved ahead to lead 5-3. I was relieved that it was the interval so raided the shelves of the nearest Boots branch, buying stuff to smell, stuff to rub on, potions, lotions, sucky sweets... You name it, I had it. If I was going to lose this match, it was going to happen on the table – and, indeed, I felt much better for the second session, which I managed to rescue by winning 5-3. We were all square at 8-8.

I then had a night to get some sleep and was raring to go the following day. I kicked off by winning the first 2 frames but he hit back with a tremendous 60-odd clearance to pinch a frame I should have had. Mark is a fantastic potter and, before I knew where I was, he was leading 12-10. That meant he just needed one more frame for the semi-final, while I had to win three. Talk about pressure... I took my usual toilet break and managed to convince myself that I was playing well and that, if he gave me any kind of opportunity, I would be able to take it. If he was going to beat me, he was going to have to earn it.

I knocked in a century to make it 12-11 and then built another good break to level things at 12-all. Now it could be anybody's match but I was determined it would be mine – I hadn't come all this way to lose in a deciding frame. There was an element of luck present but I did well to take the last frame, when I snookered him and he left me on with his escape. I held myself together really well and was delighted with my victory. I had beaten one of the great young potters, a guy who, when he tightens up his safety game, could be a future world champion.

Mark took his defeat really well. When you look at most matches played at The Crucible, the players tend not to talk to each other but I like Mark and we chatted throughout the game. When I potted the winning ball, he shook me warmly by the hand and said, 'Welcome back to the top sixteen.' I was impressed and touched that he knew how important the result was to me, and it showed more than a little bit of class. He also wanted to go and shake hands with my dad. In his post-match interview, Mark generously described my concluding three frames as 'flawless'. I wouldn't go that far but they were good.

I had secured my spot in the top 16 and felt very, very proud. When I got back to the dressing room, Dad gave me a big cuddle. It was an extremely emotional moment. I had said, after falling out of the top 16, that I didn't intend to spend more than one season in the Prestatyn qualifiers, but I'm sure that everybody who is demoted in that way says the same thing. I was fortunate it had worked out for me.

When we got back to the flat, Dad and Jim wanted to switch on the TV and watch the highlights of the game. I must admit I find that hard to do, especially during a frame where I know that I have played poorly, so I made an excuse and went to lie down. Back home, Elaine recorded the entire Championship but there are large parts I have never been able to bring myself to watch, especially later in the Championship.

I didn't want to hear any negative comments about me or my game from the television pundits, no matter how well-intentioned. Because I had played so much good snooker, I felt that Willie Thorne and company must have been saying positive things about me but I did not want to run the risk that they may have found fault with something. I am quite happy to sit there and watch other players on television but only in the background. I did pay close attention to the closing frames of the Ronnie O'Sullivan–Mark Selby quarter-final though, because I knew that I would be playing the winner.

For the semi-final I was head to head with Selby. Mark had beaten me the previous year so I wanted no repeat of that. This time around I won the first session 5-3 without playing especially well but the second session was a different matter altogether: it included my mighty break of 146. There had never been a 146 break at The Crucible before, yet in 2010 there were 2: Mark Allen's (earlier in the tournament) and mine. What are the odds of that, I wonder?

I realised early on in my break that the balls were well set. After I had potted a few reds and blacks, it crossed my mind that maybe I could record a maximum break. To do that at The Crucible would be a dream for me but, even when I ran out of position and had to pot a pink, I still realised there was a possibility of a 146, which I knew was the high break. If you cannot make a maximum, winning or sharing the high-break prize is not a bad consolation, so I decided to try and stay on the black. My position was good throughout. The money that went with it never entered my head. It was a great feeling when the final black disappeared and the crowd went mad. But I still dream of going one better and scoring a 147 break there.

Sometimes it can be really difficult to lift yourself for the next frame when you have achieved something like that, and so it turned out for me. I was 40 behind and went for a crazy plant that probably wasn't even really on and it cost me the frame. But that was the difference between the Graeme Dott who turned up at The Crucible in 2010 and the one the crowd had seen before – I had made up my mind that I was going to go for those shots.

I knew that, if I lost a frame, it didn't matter because I was certain that I would take the next. I played the same way at the UK Championship when Alex died – the commentators said that they had never seen me play at such pace and were certain it was because I had played in the Premier League, but that wasn't it at all. It had been for Alex, at a time in my life when I realised that snooker really wasn't such a very big deal – it was just a game. So yes, I had played this way before but this was different – this time I was doing it for me.

I made a couple of other decent breaks in that second session against Mark Selby and found myself 10-6 in front. I struggled in the third session of the match and I felt that I was hitting the wall. It worried me a lot because I had felt this way before when I got to both my previous finals. I would never pretend that you have to be physically fit to play snooker because that is clearly nonsense but you do have to be mentally alert.

I began to feel that there wasn't a lot left. It had all been so easy but I was starting to swim against the tide. I was leading 13-10 and was about 60 points ahead in what was the final frame of the session. Mark had already produced a couple of very good clearances to win frames he should have lost. Now he cleared the table all the way up to the pink. To win the frame he needed both the pink and black but he missed the pink. As I watched the pink roll round the angles, I remained convinced he was about to fluke it but the ball rattled in the jaws and I was able to tuck it away and lead 14-10. What a sense of relief I felt. It would have been a very different match had we gone into the final session with me leading 13-11 but now I had some breathing space.

Nevertheless, I felt that I was starting to run out of steam. Jim tried to reassure me how much I loved The Crucible and its atmosphere but, when we came back for the final session of that semi-final, I was as nervous as I have ever been on a snooker table. I don't know why but suddenly I had all these horrible, negative thoughts going through my head. I had started to lose position and I knew that Mark was at his best when he was behind. There was no doubt in my mind that he was going to come out and play really well but I didn't know if I had enough left in the tank to cope with what he might throw at me.

Despite what I was feeling inside, I desperately wanted to beat Mark and reach a World Championship final for the third time. When I reached my first final, I know that some people thought I'd never make it to another one. I shocked them when I got back there again – and I stunned them when I won it. To make a third final after everything that I had been through was beyond my wildest dreams. There are not many snooker players who reach the final of the World Championship three times and there are even fewer who do it three times in six years.

I have been guilty at various times in my career of not setting my goals high enough. I would sit down at the start of a season and tell myself that I just wanted to stay in the top 16 and I believe that your brain can kind of switch off if you don't set lofty goals. I should have been telling myself that I wanted to be in the top 4 and, by doing that, I may only have got to No. 7 or 8 but it would have been better than finishing the year as the world's 15th-best snooker player.

I had arrived at Sheffield in 2010 believing that I could beat anybody, given the opportunity. So yes, the final session against Mark was tough and he did exactly as I thought he would, winning the first 3 frames to make it 14-13. I then knocked in a 40-odd break, which was probably the best of the tournament in as much as I was never in position and I kept knocking in impossible shots. During that break I thought to myself, You should be playing safe here but you have got to show Mark you are still here, still fighting and still competing. I kept taking on the pots and they kept disappearing. It was exhilarating but it was also exhausting.

My confidence was starting to pay off in a big way. I felt liberated. Every red I took on seemed to disappear into the pocket. Nobody could possibly call me a grinder now and even my biggest detractors would surely have to admit a sneaky admiration for what I was doing. I felt that I had become an entertainer, as if I was Jimmy White in his heyday. It might not have looked like that to others but, in my head, it did.

I was trying to show Mark Selby that, although he had won three frames on the bounce, I was still OK. Who was I kidding? But I was now 15-13 up. You always want to finish off a match in style, perhaps with a couple of big breaks, but sometimes you have to take whatever comes your way. Eventually I won 17-14 and, against all the odds, I was back in the final again. I know that, on paper, it looked like I coasted past Peter Ebdon and Stephen Maguire but those matches took as much out of me as did beating Mark Allen and Mark Selby. Deep down I thrive on everything that the World Championship throws at me. It's because of the ability I have to feed off the atmosphere that I manage to hang in there.

After beating Mark Selby, I then had to do a series of interviews and somebody from the WSA advised me beforehand that a story was going to break in the following day's newspapers. There had been an ongoing police inquiry into a match involving Jamie Burnett and Stephen Maguire and I thought that, perhaps, a decision had finally been reached on whether or not charges were going to be brought against them. But I was told it wasn't that. In the end, I was only questioned about my match with Selby and about my prospects for the final.

I had finished my semi-final at about 11.30pm but I didn't get to bed until about 2am. Each player gets ten tickets and ten backstage passes, so I had to make the arrangements for all my friends and family who had been in touch to tell me they were going to come down to Sheffield for the final. The passes get people into every part of The Crucible. In the end, I had about 15 people coming down to watch me. There was

Elaine and our kids, Elaine's sister and her husband and their kids, my mum, my brothers, their families, Alex Junior and a friend of his.

I don't have a problem with any of that. I love the fact that they all want to cheer me on and be part of it. The problem with it is that the arrangements are all very last minute; it is generally down to me to organise the tickets and that is hardly ideal with a final coming up. There are also hotels to be booked and that is always easier said than done in Sheffield during the weekend of the final, which always also falls on a Bank Holiday. Thankfully, Jim was brilliant and he stepped up to the plate. I gave him a list of everybody who was coming and he set about arranging hotel rooms for them all. His wife Shirley came down so he ended up moving into a hotel with her, while Dad moved into another hotel with one of my brothers so that Elaine and the children could join me in the flat. It was like a complicated game of musical chairs but I cannot express how much I appreciated the efforts of all those involved.

We had also logged on to the internet when we got back to the flat and that was when I first became aware of the *News of the World* story alleging that John Higgins and his manager Pat Mooney (who was also my manager) had agreed to throw a frame in return for cash. I was stunned – although both were eventually cleared of match fixing, Higgins was fined and suspended for six months for failing to report that he had been approached and Mooney was permanently suspended from the WPBSA. It was hardly the perfect way to prepare for a final as I knew it was the only thing the media would be talking about, as well as the main topic of conversation among those who had paid to come and watch that final.

There have been numerous accusations made against several players but I can say that I truly believe the sport of snooker to be one of the cleanest. There have definitely been some dodgy goings-on in tennis and cricket, and it would surprise me if football in the lower leagues was not affected by the odd betting scam. But nobody has ever approached me to throw a frame or a match. If they did, I would report them straight away.

Having got to bed at 2am that Saturday night, it was at least another two hours before I finally dropped off. The Higgins story in the paper was not the reason that I was unable to sleep though. It was because I was on such a high after my semi-final win. I woke up at dawn, knowing that I had 16 frames of snooker in front of me that day – and possibly a further 19 on the Monday.

My opponent in the 2010 World Championship final was Neil Robertson, the Australian. I played OK during the first session on the Sunday afternoon but my energy was flagging and I had told Jim that I was going to continue going for every ball. 'I don't think I can be here long,' I said. 'One way or another, I need to get this done quickly.' Neil had other ideas; he wanted to slow everything down and make it a tactical game. It was completely the reverse of the match we had played in 2006, when he was the one who was aiming for all-out attack and I was the one who wanted to slow it down.

It was the first time Robertson had been in the world final though, and nerves may have played a part. Whatever the reason, the frames were scrappy, there was little or no fluency from either of us and it wasn't a good match to watch or to be involved in, although Neil would probably disagree.

The first session should have kicked off at 3pm, which is too late anyway, but, because the BBC had been discussing the allegations involving John Higgins, we didn't begin until nearly 3.30pm. We had started late because the BBC had been discussing the allegations involving John Higgins in depth. I did not want to comment on the story at time and I still find it difficult to take it in, as John is one of the straightest guys you could ever wish to meet.

I would never use any of this as an excuse for the way I played in the final but it certainly didn't help us. In some respects it was just as well that the match wasn't a classic because, even if it had been, 2010 would always be remembered as the year Higgins was accused of match fixing. After the first session, which I won 5-3, I just about had time to go back to the flat and get something to eat and then I had to return. I had got through the first frames on adrenalin but that can only keep you going for so long.

I was as flat as a pancake when I returned for the second session and so was my snooker. I have hit the wall many times but this was easily the worst. I had nothing left to draw upon. I sat there thinking that I was not going to win a frame, no matter where he left the balls. In the end I lost it 6-2 and thought it was a miracle that I won 2 frames. So I was 9-7 down overall but I tried to reassure myself that all was not lost and that I couldn't possibly feel this bad the next day. So the plan was to get to bed and have a good night's sleep. I wasn't due back in the arena until the Monday afternoon so I could even have a lie-in.

I got up on Monday at 10am. Lewis, my young son, was in the flat so I decided to take him down to The Crucible while I got on the practice table and, maybe, I could take some pictures of him. After all, I might never be in this position again. He was just about tall enough to reach the table and re-spot the black ball for me and that is what he did. He was really excited to be part of it all, especially when I showed him around the place, telling him where the commentators sat. Then I took him into the arena and showed where I walked through the curtain when my name was announced, the table and my seat. I even let him climb the ladder into the TV commentary box and took pictures of him sitting in my seat. He loved it all and it helped to put things into perspective for me: when all is said and done, I play this game to provide for my family.

Back at school, Lewis would love it when his friends told him that they had seen his daddy on TV. It made him feel special. We had taken a conscious decision to send Lewis to a state-run primary school because we want him to have an ordinary life. His friends are his friends because of who he is, not because his father is a former world snooker champion and, when they come to our house to play with him, I hardly get a second look, which is exactly the way it should be. It will be the same with Lucy as she gets older.

When play got underway for the final's second day on the Monday afternoon, I felt fresher than I had the previous day. Sadly, it is impossible to say the same thing about the standard of snooker Neil and I played. Every time I thought I was going to get back into it, I would lose another frame and, because the play was so scrappy, we did not play the full eight frames. They told us that they wanted to take us off so that we could go away and have a proper meal before the last session got under way. It made no sense to me. Why would you start the session at 3pm in the first place? Asking players to complete eight frames with such a late starting time is asking too much and it was inevitable that there was going to be another late finish. When we were taken off, Neil led 12-10, miles away from the winning line for both of us. I had to win eight more frames, while he still required six. There were a possible 13 frames of snooker still to be played.

Going into the final, I'd recorded eight century breaks, the most of any player in Sheffield, but whatever magic there had been in my cue had well and truly got up and gone home by now. The two of us continued to struggle, playing scrappy frames and getting involved in dour safety battles. If it wasn't good to watch – and I know that it wasn't – I can assure you that it wasn't any better to be a part of. I am pretty sure people would have looked at the two of us beforehand and, having seen all the breaks we had made on the way to the final, would have been looking forward to a final that would feature lots of sizeable breaks.

Neil and I shared the first 4 frames in the evening so the score was now 14-12. During the interval I once again told Jim that I was spent. 'I am not saying that I am beaten but I am done in,' I told him.

'Come on, Graeme,' said Jim. 'If you can just win this first frame and make it 14-13 and then maybe pinch the next one, you can still win this thing.'

I have never quit in my entire life but this feeling of exhaustion was like nothing I had ever experienced before. I did pull one frame back to make it 14-13 but then Neil won a big frame on the pink ball to make the score 15-13, so now he only required 3 more frames to become world champion.

In the 29th frame Neil was on a decent break. Watching him, I thought that I could have given up there and then. I don't wear a watch when I play snooker because I find it uncomfortable but I knew that it was at least 11pm. I've got 13 frames, which means I've got to win 5 more if I want the title. I knew that I was in no shape to knock in any century breaks – the only way I could win a frame was with perhaps two 40-odd breaks and a safety battle, and I didn't have it in me to achieve that. I could have been there for, perhaps, another three hours, assuming that Neil didn't win any more frames. Who would want to watch us still playing at 2am?

When a battler like me considers giving up in a final, it makes that final something of a farce. I am not saying that I would ever have quit, of course, but the circumstances of the match – all the stopping and starting, the fact that neither of us was playing fluently – meant that the thought was in my head. I could easily have walked over to Neil and said, 'I accept you have won. I just can't play any more.'

I had felt the same way in my match against Peter Ebdon but, at least on that occasion, the finishing line was in sight for me and I knew that I could get there. Against Neil I felt a million miles away from the end. The thing is that, at 15-13, I was still bang in the match, on paper at least.

I had gone into the final convinced that it would be a potting extravaganza but nothing could have been further form the truth in the end. No matter how many positives I tried to find, I was aware that the crowd at The Crucible and the TV fans at home could not possibly be enjoying it. At least the people at home could switch off their television sets and I am sure that many of them did. I wanted to make the game better but there was nothing I could do. There were quite a few empty seats in the arena by now, so I assumed that some were so disgusted at the quality of the game that they'd walked out. In fact, many of them had just gone out into the foyer to watch it on television, where they could stretch their legs and make a quick getaway when it finally ended.

Every time I got to the table I was still trying to pot every ball and I gave it a hundred per cent but there was nothing there for me. If I potted a great red, there was no colour on. The harder I tried, the worse it got. Then, finally, Neil put me out of my misery, winning 18-13. I shook his hand and felt relieved it was all over.

It was not a vintage final. It ended at 12.54am on Tuesday morning. Over the two days, we had managed only one century break between us, and at one point Neil took 4 minutes and 40 seconds deciding whether or not to put me back in after I had played a foul. And those were the highlights! It hurt me to see Neil pick up the trophy but he had played better than me and deserved to be world champion. But I was able to think, Well, at least my name is on it. It's his time to win it. He is going to take that home tonight but my name is still on it.

The match may have been over but there was still the post-match interview to go through – easy enough when you've won. Such interviews must have been torture for Jimmy White, who had to cope with six of them over the years – one for each final he lost. Next there were all the national newspaper interviews to do and then the drug test. After all of that there is a party, attended by all the players, officials, TV commentators and suchlike. It is held at a hotel not far from

The Crucible and, when you have just been beaten in the final, it is not really somewhere that you want to be. I received cufflinks as a memento and stayed just long enough to hear Neil's winning speech.

I told John Virgo how tired I was. 'No wonder you're tired,' he replied. 'Who wouldn't be? To win that title, Graeme, you would have had to play until three in the morning.' It was my cue to leave – everybody commented on how tired I must have been. I blamed the scheduling but then thought that maybe I just have a problem with stamina, although I much prefer the longer match format at Sheffield.

Then I reflected on other World Championship finals at The Crucible. John Higgins versus Mark Selby in 2007, for instance, should have been a classic but it wasn't: John built up a big lead but then he, too, hit the wall and fell over the line. I spoke to John about it and he told me that he felt exactly the same way that I did when I beat Peter Ebdon.

If you look through the record books, you will struggle to find a final where both men played well, yet there have been so many classic semi-finals. I had great semis against Matthew Stevens, Ronnie O'Sullivan and Mark Selby but it just seems that the final is a match too far. As I said earlier, maybe a rest day for the finalists or the introduction of a third-place playoff would take the heat off the finalists. There is nothing wrong with the idea of giving the finalists a day off – they do it at Wimbledon. Yes, I know that tennis players go through far more physical exertion but I hope by now that I've clarified just how much of a toll these gruelling snooker matches have on the mind. I'm not a lone voice on this one – most players feel the same way.

Serving up second-rate snooker from over-tired players is neither good for the sport nor for the BBC's coverage. If people tune in and see a great final it will encourage them to take up the game. And the final does not have to be over two days. Make it the first player to 15 and have a session in the morning, a session in the afternoon and a session in the evening. In saying all of that, if the governing body didn't change a thing, I would still quite happily play in the final every year because I love The Crucible and the whole idea of the World Championship so much.

When I returned from Sheffield to Larkhall, people were genuinely pleased that I had reached the final and regained my world ranking but there were no banners or parties this time. That was fine with me – that's the way I like it. I just wanted to come back and sneak into the house without any fuss.

There was one bit of unfinished business that I wasn't looking forward to. With Pat Mooney and John Higgins both suspended, I had to phone Pat and tell him he could no longer be my manager, but Pat made it easy for me. 'I know why you are phoning me, Graeme, but the way things are at present, I can no longer manage you anyway. I am no longer able to be involved in snooker.' It was a shame because I liked the man but that's the way it had to be so now I am managing myself again.

There was another significant event in our lives in 2010 – we had to find new homes for Sasha and Buster, our beloved Labradors. It broke my heart. The dogs had gone from having the run of the entire house to being restricted to the kitchen. Elaine had two young children and two large, energetic dogs to look after, as well as keeping a house going and it was unfair. When she told me it was getting too much, I found it hard to accept but I knew that the dogs had to go. They are now with a new family, which loves them and gives them all the exercise they require.

We have had other pets since the children came along but I think it is fair to say that we haven't had much luck with them. Or, to be more accurate, the pets haven't had much luck with us. We bought goldfish – they died, as did their replacements. Then there was a guinea pig that Lewis and I loved but it seemed every time you just looked at this animal it did the toilet. I couldn't believe that this was normal but then I got on the internet and realised that a guinea pig can drop 50 pellets a day. I used to put it on my shoulder and it would pee on me. We kept it in the kitchen and I seemed to spend my life cleaning its cage and spraying air freshener in the kitchen, so it was taken back to the pet shop.

Apart from a couple of charity golf days during the summer of 2010, I spent the time recharging my batteries and getting ready for the season that lay ahead. There are going to be some big changes in my sport.

Take the rankings, for instance. They have always been done on a two-year basis so, if you have a poor season, the chances are that you will remain in the top 16, but there will now be three times during the season when players are re-ranked. At the start of the 2010–11 season I knew that I would not have to pre-qualify for the World Open or the China Open, but there are now a series of smaller events, mainly played over the best of five frames, and they also count towards the world ranking. It is extremely complicated but, after the World Open and the China Open, we were all given a new ranking, which meant it was possible that I could then fall out of the top 16 and would have to pre-qualify for the next tournaments. The whole process would happen again after the UK Championship and a new tournament – the German Open. So it all meant that I began the season not certain that I would have an automatic place at The Crucible in April 2011.

Barry Hearn set up the German Open. I've already described how much the Chinese love their snooker but the Germans are also fanatics. They just can't get enough of the game. I have played in Germany before, in a competition organised by Pat Mooney, and beat Shaun Murphy in the final in front of a passionate crowd of 2,000 people. It was fantastic.

I know that Barry will try new things and not all will work. Take the World Open, held at the Scottish Exhibition Centre in September 2010. With all matches up to the final being the best of five, I know that Barry envisaged it being a crash-bang-wallop tournament with lots of fast and furious snooker but, in practice, players were petrified of making mistakes. They didn't want to lose a single frame because they knew that, if the winner was the first player to get to three, there was no margin for error. The result was lots of really dull frames that took 30-40 minutes, which I'd imagine was not what Barry – or anybody else – was looking for. My involvement in the World Open ended in the third round, when I lost 3-1 to Neil Robertson and I felt that I hadn't had time to get the pace of the table or a feel for the atmosphere.

I worry constantly about keeping my place in the upper

echelons of the game. I know what it is like to endure a slump, to go through a period when you don't win matches or earn money (as also happened to a good friend of mine, Billy Snaddon, when he lost his form), and I don't ever want to go through it again. Remember that professional snooker players do not receive any money after the World Championship is over (at the start of May) until the first tournament of the following season (in late August). Imagine how difficult that can be if you're not in the top 16 and, even if you are, you could get knocked out in the first round of a tournament and receive a cheque for only £2,000.

There is no contingency plan. If it all ended for me, I do not have the foggiest idea what I would do with the rest of my life. I have given it a great deal of thought but snooker is all that I know. I guess it means that I just need to keep on winning. My one wish is that, when the time comes when either snooker is finished with me or I am done with it, I will have enough money. Right now, I am nowhere near where I would like to be. Obviously, I have the house bought and paid for so, if the absolute worst came to the worst, we could sell it. In my heart, I would love to have a business of my own – something that would earn me a wage – but I don't have the first idea what that business might be.

One option, I suppose, is to play exhibitions. When I have done them I've enjoyed them. John Higgins and I have done a few of them, where we have played best-of-nine matches, and we have had a laugh with one another and tried to get the crowd involved. We would finish it off by playing a couple of frames with the locals. That was fun but the thought of routinely going around the country to play a few frames of snooker – at what could be a dreadful venue for just a few hundred pounds – is not especially appealing.

I am not knocking the guys who regularly play exhibitions but, given the choice, I would rather play on my own table during the day and spend the evenings with my family. It took me a long while to reclaim my hunger for the game but stepping on the exhibition treadmill could mean that I might lose that hunger again. In the future, who knows?

CHAPTER TWENTY-ONE

FADS AND PHASES

I am probably the laziest person I know. I would quite happily sit all day in front of the TV, especially on a Saturday, when Elaine announced that she was taking the kids out or was going to see a friend and I could watch the horse racing, the football and some American golf. With Sky TV you can watch European golf during the day and then go straight onto the PGA Tour golf. Bliss. I should stress, though, that I don't get the chance to do that any longer: the children come first.

I suppose that, because I am so inactive, I tend to feel quite tired a lot of the time but it was my mum who told me I should get up off my backside and do something about it. But I couldn't just buy a cheap exercise machine. Oh no – I had to buy the full multi-gym experience. It cost me a fortune and I even managed to use it once or twice but, three weeks later, I was hanging clothes on it so I had to give it away.

I came to the conclusion that I needed to get fit by taking up running so I started jogging around the streets of Larkhall. The problem with that was that I kept bumping into people I knew and they wanted to stop and have a chat. And there was also the weather – it is not a lot of fun running along when you've got the rain and sleet driving into your face. Plus, I was also experiencing some pain in my shins, which I didn't much enjoy, so I'd go to a park and run around the grass. I stuck that for a while but then I'd lose in the first round of a tournament and think, What's the point of all this keep-fit nonsense? It was supposed to make me sharper but now I can't win a match.

I convinced myself I didn't enjoy running because I was outside doing it. I knew that, if I could watch the TV while I was running, I would get into it, sharpen up my fitness and stamina, and beat everybody out of sight. So I bought myself a treadmill – obviously a top-of-the-range treadmill with all the bells and whistles, which wouldn't have looked out of place in a proper gym. The day it was delivered, it took three guys to drag it in to the house but they left it downstairs and cleared off.

After they had gone, I decided that I really wanted the treadmill upstairs, perhaps in the bedroom. Surely Elaine wouldn't mind. She would be delighted that I was making an effort to get fit. Jim offered to help me carry it upstairs but you should have seen his face when he arrived and saw how big it was. He managed to move it, though, as I pretended to help. Then we got it all wired up and plugged in.

I started using it and there I was pounding away, trying to convince myself that I was enjoying it. To be fair, I persevered for all of, oh, a month. Elaine hated it being in the bedroom but I couldn't face the thought of asking Jim to move it back downstairs again. Eventually she moaned so much that I told her we should just give the thing away. A friend's husband decided it was just the job, especially when he was getting it for nothing – but I made sure I was out when he came to collect it. Elaine now regrets telling me that the treadmill had to go as she has started going to the gym and has become totally hooked. I would love to go to the gym with her, of course, but somebody has to stay at home and look after the children.

For me, when I go out to buy something, it always has to be the best or nothing. If I were to take up chess, I would go out and buy the most expensive chess set on the market, only to discover after a week that I hated the game, then chess pieces would start to go missing. The obvious, sensible thing would be to buy a portable chess set and then progress to something better. But I have never been able to do that.

CHAPTER TWENTY-TWO
THE FIRE WITHIN

I am quite a competitive person and that manifests itself not only in my snooker but also in my golf. It's a game that I love but anybody who has ever played will know just how frustrating it can be. Golf is a game that keeps bringing you back. Everybody who plays it wants to get better and will, at some stage, convince themselves that they have found the secret to the game. I am no exception.

During the summer of 2010 I managed to get my handicap down to six. I don't hit the ball miles but I hit it fairly straight. Unlike most snooker players, my weakness is my putting. I don't know why that should be – as everyone tells me, seeing as I spend my professional life hitting balls into pockets, that I should be able to transfer that skill to the golf course. I can see the logic but the technique is completely different. Well, that's my story and I'm sticking to it.

I play at a golf course in Hamilton with Jim (who has a

handicap of ten) and, throughout the summer of 2010, I was scoring really well. A bad round for me would be no worse than, say, nine over par and, quite often, I was going round the course in two or three over par. My mind started to wander and I told Jim that there were several forthcoming competitions where we could do well. The big competition at our club is called The Silver Grouse and it is for golfers with handicaps from 6 to 12. I told Jim there was no reason why one or other of us couldn't win it.

It's a 36-hole competition, with one round in the morning and another in the afternoon. I had been placed third a couple of years earlier but, come the big day this year, I was atrocious. I dropped a shot at the first hole, missing a tiny putt in the process. I wasn't too worried – there were 35 holes to go, 35 chances to get it right, but a few holes later I missed another short putt. By the time we had completed the first round I had missed a total of five putts of three feet or less. I was not in a good mood.

I had shot an 81 and, as Jim and I sat in the car having our lunch, I was quietly raging away inside. I had thrown away the chance of a good round. If you play golf, you will know that, when one part of your game starts to go wrong, it has a habit of feeding into other areas. I had spent weeks looking forward to this competition but I had blown it and my head was gone. Jim hadn't played well either but he is more able to take disappointment in his stride.

I should explain that we were playing with a third golfer, a pleasant enough man we had never met in competition before. One of the great things about golf is that it gives you the opportunity to meet new people – although I am sure that by the time this day was out he wasn't feeling that way. Before we teed off in the afternoon I thought, This guy must think I'm rubbish. He hasn't seen me hole a single decent putt all morning. It's embarrassing.

I convinced myself that I couldn't get any worse and, fortunately, I played the first four holes pretty well. This was more like it. Then we got to the fifth hole and I missed another three-foot putt. I may have been using my favourite putter but today it was pushing its luck!

At the eighth hole, which has a pond beside the green, I had left myself another short one. Before I hit the ball I told Jim, 'If I miss this putt, the club is going in the water.' He told me not to be so stupid – but it worked and I holed the putt. I missed another tiddler at the 9th hole and, at the 10th, I was 25 feet from the hole and left my first effort a good 12 feet short. It was the last straw. I three-putted, turned round and threw my putter as hard and as far as I could. It vanished into the undergrowth amid the trees not far from the green.

Jim burst out laughing but our playing partner told me to go and get my putter. When I refused, he said that he would go and fetch it instead. I was trying to be nonchalant, acting as if it didn't bother me but, deep down, I was cringing with embarrassment: it had occurred to me that I was ruining his day, not just mine.

'No, seriously,' I insisted. 'Just leave it. It's probably stuck up a tree. I never want to see it again. I'm not bothered.' But I *was* bothered. I resorted to finishing the round with a variety of clubs.

At home, Elaine wasn't terribly impressed at what I'd done.

'You are like a child,' she said. 'It's only a game and you are supposed to be out there enjoying yourself.'

She was right, of course, and I had to reconsider what I'd done. 'That's a good putter I've thrown away. It's a Ping and it cost me a lot of money.'

I told Elaine I was popping out for a few minutes. I went back to the golf course but to get to the tenth hole I had to walk across the course so, if there was anybody else about, they would see me. I tried to sneak on but, as I was walking across the 11th fairway, there were 3 golfers and I had no choice but to say hello to them. I could feel their eyes following me, wondering what on earth I was up to.

When I reached the trees, I started rummaging around. How difficult could it be to find a putter? Eventually I stumbled across it but, by the time I got back to the 14th fairway on my way back to the car, the same 3 guys were playing the hole. They had seen me walking one way with nothing in my hands and now I was heading back carrying a putter.

'Aye, you must have had a bad day right enough if you are throwing your putter away,' one of them shouted. Like Jim earlier, they all had a good laugh at my expense and I couldn't blame them. I was red faced and very embarrassed again. So did the putter go back in my bag? Don't be daft. I went out and bought another one. That should teach it a lesson.

Most professional sportsmen are competitive at whatever they do. I guess it is part and parcel of what makes you successful in the first place. If you didn't care, how could you motivate yourself to win?

CHAPTER TWENTY-THREE

BEST OF
THE REST

*T*his book gives me a unique opportunity to share my thoughts with you about a few of my fellow professionals, so here goes...

RONNIE O'SULLIVAN

We have never been what you what call bosom buddies but, when I was in the depths of my battle with depression, he phoned me to see how I was and to share his experiences of the condition.

I was deeply touched by the gesture because it was something that he didn't need to do. He had nothing to gain by doing it because nobody was going to know. He told me about some of the things that he had been through and it helped me to hear his side of things. Depression affects people in different ways and I know he struggled terribly with it but this was a selfless gesture and he went way up in my estimation as a result of that one simple phone call. It was a classy thing to do. Sometimes that is all it takes to change your opinion about a person.

As a snooker player, Ronnie is in a class of one. He can play shots and make breaks that the rest of us can only dream about but there are times when you play him and you quickly realise that he would rather be anywhere else than in an arena playing snooker. Because I have been through depression, I look at some of the things he does and can understand why he has done them. It should never be forgotten that he has been through a great deal off the table, coping with his father spending all those years in jail for murder, as well as his mother also going to prison.

Sometimes I think he might have benefitted from taking some time away from the game to get his head right but only Ronnie knows whether that is true or not. He is too good a player to be remembered for walking out of a match against Stephen Hendry at the UK Championship or for telling the press that he hates the game. He keeps himself to himself at times and, again, I can relate to that – when I was feeling at my lowest, I didn't want to mix with other people.

There are also times when I feel that the media bait Ronnie in an effort to get him to say something controversial and he is the type of man who, more often than not, will oblige and away they go, rubbing their hands together in glee.

To focus on the positives, though, he's breathtaking to watch sometimes, especially the way that he can flit between playing with his left and his right hand. He is a genius but sometimes he looks a bit lost.

STEPHEN HENDRY

The best there has ever been, no question. Some people say that Ronnie is equally good – and he is obviously the most naturally-gifted player we have seen – but Stephen has won more titles and has taken the game to a different level. He raised the bar and showed the guys who came along afterwards what they had to do.

Even though Stephen has won everything there is to win in the game, I believe that he is still desperate to win more titles. He remains a formidable break-builder but, these days, he tends to make more mistakes in a single match than he used to during an entire season. He says that he is as good as ever in practice but I sense that, when sportsmen reach a certain age, it becomes increasingly difficult to motivate and maintain that killer edge. Perhaps Stephen has reached that age.

The game has also moved on. Just as tournaments were dominated by Ray Reardon in the 1970s and Steve Davis in the 1980s, Hendry was the daddy in the 1990s. During that decade's run of World Championships, you could have Hendry in one half of the draw and Jimmy White in the other – and you could bet your house on the likelihood of them meeting in the final; it happened six times. You couldn't do that with any degree of certainty today. Everybody who enters a tournament today is capable of winning it and it's very unusual now to see one player win two events in a season. While Hendry was at the top of his game he was winning three and four titles a year.

Whereas Steve Davis continues to compete despite his slide down the rankings, I cannot believe that Stephen will do the same. When he drops out of the top 16 I'm not sure we will see him playing the game again. That way, people will remember him for the great player he was.

STEPHEN MAGUIRE

What can I say about my fellow Scot other than that he is another great, near-faultless player? In truth, even he would probably admit that he should have won more than he has but some players burst on the scene and start winning almost immediately, as he did, and then take a while to get back to that level.

He had a match-fixing allegation hanging over his head for far too long and it clearly got into his head and affected his game. When his head is right, he is as good as anybody. He is a very similar player to Hendry at his best. He scores heavily and tries to bully his opponents. On top of that, he has a tremendous safety game and great bottle.

MATTHEW STEVENS

For a while Matthew looked to be unbeatable. While we are not close friends, we get on well. His dad used to go everywhere with him, so Matthew must have found it difficult when his father died. He has never come out and said anything to that effect in public but I don't see how you can have that sort of relationship with somebody and carry on as normal after they die.

I know how it affected me when Alex, my manager, passed away. For Matthew, his father could have been a highly motivating force in his game and it's hard to fill the gap when that motivating force is no longer present.

However, there have been signs that he is on the way back and snooker would be a better place for having him back in the top 16 – which is surely where he belongs.

MARK SELBY

Of all the players who have yet to win the World Championship, Mark is best equipped to do it. He has the perfect game for the marathon that is the World Championship. He possesses a really solid safety game and scores as heavily as anyone when he gets in. He never has a really bad session and, like all the top players, has plenty of bottle.

JOHN HIGGINS

John has been a close friend for more than four years and I was stunned when he was accused of being prepared to take money in return for throwing some frames of snooker. That wasn't the man I knew. Although he was eventually cleared, he received a six-month ban and a £75,000 fine. I know how worried he has been about how fans and fellow players might treat him on his return to the game.

John has the best all-round game in the world, other than Ronnie at his absolute best. Even on a bad day for John, you still have to be at your very best to beat him and that is easily his best trait. He just won't go away and never knows when he is beaten.

DING JUNHUI

He keeps himself to himself so I don't know much about him but we were all stunned when he was in tears after losing to Ronnie in the 2007 Masters final at Wembley. While he is a tremendous potter who is capable of scoring very heavily, there are question marks over his temperament.

His poor record in the World Championships is a big surprise to me. If he is not firing on all cylinders, there are times when he seems to give up and you certainly can't do that at The Crucible. But he certainly has the talent and there is no reason why he should not be a future world champion.

MARK ALLEN

Seems to keep improving parts of his game all the time. Has a great attitude and as far potting and break building goes he is as good as anyone. It was always his tactical play that let him down but I could see first-hand when we played in the quarter-final in 2010 that he had been working on that. His safety play was immense, and when he gets the balance right he will be a force in the game of snooker for a very long time. On top of all that, he is a down to earth young man and is one of the game's good guys.

NEIL ROBERTSON

The Australian is a worthy world champion and he beat me fair and square at The Crucible in 2010. When he first burst onto the scene he was a player who went for everything; a real breath of fresh air. Obviously you can't continue like that – sometimes you need to rein in your attacking instincts.

Neil obviously realised that he couldn't continue trying to pot every ball and the fact that he became world champion proves he was correct, but I believe he has gone too far the other way and that he sometimes plays too conservatively. When he gets the balance right – and I reckon that he probably will – he could become a very difficult man to beat.

MARK WILLIAMS

Mark was in the doldrums for a few years and it is great to see him back where he belongs. He is the best single-ball potter in the game and also has the best attitude – no matter how poorly he is playing, he can blank it out and make a century. Mark is probably my favourite player to watch when he is in full flow.

SHAUN MURPHY

In my view, he has the best cue action in the game and played some of the best snooker that I have ever seen when he won the World Championship. He is a great ambassador for our sport, says all the right things and when he does lose he always takes it on the chin and makes no excuses. A true gent.

Who, or what, is next?
There are bound to be some up-and-coming teenagers who will take the sport by storm but I do worry about the future

of the game. At one time in Scotland it seemed that we had a never-ending production line that just kept turning out great young players. Sadly, it seems to me that the allure of computer games is now too great and that kids are just happy to sit at home and play them.

I would love to see the Scottish Parliament funding a snooker academy and it is something I would be interested in getting involved with. The sort of thing I have in mind would provide kids with an education as well as top-level coaching. Players such as myself, Alan McManus and Stephen Hendry could go along and help them with not only the tactical side of snooker, but we would also be able to share our experiences with them.

There is already an academy in Sheffield but I don't believe it is enough. Other sports, such as golf, cricket and tennis, get into schools and give kids taster sessions. It is only by doing that that we will get them hooked and identify the stars of tomorrow. The Scottish Parliament could afford to fund such a project but will it ever happen? I doubt it.

Some kids give up because they don't get the right sort of coaching. They reach a certain level and then there is nobody to take them to the next level. That is where an academy could make a huge difference. Talent scouts in Scotland could attend junior tournaments and identify the best young players. Those youngsters would then be brought under the umbrella of the academy and would receive the best coaching and the best advice.

At present, a good young player has nowhere to go other than to a snooker club, leaving his parents to fork out a lot of money to pay for his table time, to get him to tournaments and suchlike. If the academy took those youngsters under its wing, the pressure would be off the parents and the boys would be free to develop. It costs about £6 an hour to play on a snooker table in a club and for many families that is a lot of money, especially when you consider that, in order to improve their game, the boy may want to play for anything up to four hours a day, every day of the week. You do the maths.

If my parents hadn't been prepared to scrape the money together and if Uncle George hadn't received his redundancy money, I might have ended up following a very different route. And then, of course, I had a mentor like Alex. But I was lucky. There might be good talent out there but we still have to unearth it. What is needed is a benefactor – somebody with deep pockets and a love of the game.

CHAPTER TWENTY-FOUR

AND FINALLY...

All that I really want for the future is to know that everybody I am close to remains fit and healthy. I have experienced more than my fair share of heartache, as have the people I care about, and it would be fantastic to have some respite. I know that people would expect me to say that I want to win the World Championship again and become No. 1 in the world. Obviously that would be great but such things are meaningless without personal happiness and contentment.

I want Elaine and the children to be well and happy, as well as my parents, young Alex, Jim, George and their families. I am not a greedy man. As far as my career is concerned, I know that I am not going to win seven world titles and I will settle for simply being allowed to compete for titles and earning enough to ensure that my family is comfortable. I will continue to work hard at my game and, hopefully, I will be rewarded for that. I believe that you get back from life what you put in. If you keep knocking at the door, you will eventually be allowed in. And it would be nice to be thought of as a decent human being.

The whole fame thing is odd. I do not regard myself as special in any way. I am just a guy who happens to be able to play snooker. There are some sportsmen who love the idea of being hero worshipped but that is not me. I find it hard to think of myself as a celebrity – when I am invited to Celeb-Am golf days, I tend to tell my friends that I've been invited to play in a pro-am.

But I don't have a problem with people recognising me and asking for autographs. It would be rude to tell a fan that I was too busy to give them a few seconds of my time, especially because they would have already made up their mind that they liked me. I would hate to spoil that feeling. Of course, there are times when you would rather be left alone but you can't let people know that.

One year at The Crucible I decided to sign every programme, every piece of paper and every autograph book. If I did it once, I wouldn't have to do it again. How wrong could I be? The very next time I approached the theatre, there was another queue of people and I swear that many of them had already asked me. What I tend to do now in Sheffield is to sign autographs while I am walking – apart from anything else, the weather is often pretty miserable, so you really don't want to be standing outside. Some players get asked to sign girls' breasts but the strangest thing I have ever been asked to sign is somebody's arm.

I will often be out with Elaine and will see people nudging

each other and hear, 'That's Graeme Dott, the snooker player.' It is not a big deal. Yes, I am in the public eye and with that come certain responsibilities but I don't drink so I don't have to worry about going out for a night and making a fool of myself.

The best life advice I got was when I was told to treat other people the way I would like to be treated myself. It's just one of the reasons why I always make time for fans. Somebody else told me that you need to look after people when you are on the way up the ladder because it is a racing certainty that you will bump into them again when you are on the way down.

I don't want anybody to take this the wrong way but I don't believe there is anybody that knows me who could genuinely say that they don't like me. There may be people who have watched me play snooker on TV and don't like the way I play but, if I was asked to name my best trait, it would be that I was brought up to respect people. Of course, there are some who rub you up the wrong way – I have mentioned a couple of them in this book. But that is human nature.

The best snooker advice I ever got was from a Scottish player called John Lardner. He said, 'When you lose a really bad frame, you should always try your nuts off to win the next one because it will really bug your opponent.' I didn't know what he meant until much later: a bad frame was one where your opponent has, perhaps, needed a snooker and has managed to get it and gone on to win the frame. He would be ecstatic because he would be convinced that he had really hurt you.

Lardner's view was that, if you came straight back and won the next frame, it would leave your opponent feeling pretty demoralised, wondering what he had to do to beat you.

And I tell you, Lardner was right.

WORLD SNOOKER CHAMPION 2006

GRAEME DOTT

He travelled to Sheffield,
A man on a mission,
To be World Snooker Champion,
His greatest ambition.
From the first round,
He matched the elite,
Kept the viewers spellbound,
Every game was a treat.
John Parrot, Nigel Bond,
He put to the test,
Neil Robertson, Ronnie O,
Now, his chance to be best.
Came the final with Ebdon,
They were two of a kind,

Steely, tenacious,
Both of the one mind.
To win that top prize,
The goal of each man,
To make their family proud,
And please every fan,
In that marathon game,
One thought in his head,
Just win one more frame,
To stay in the lead.
Then – A remarkable clearance
In game thirty-one,
He roared like a lion,
Knowing he'd won,
Tactical, Formidable,
The odds eighty to one,
Graeme Dott left the Crucible,
Second to none.

By Rita Little